THE ACADEMIC MAN
IN THE CATHOLIC COLLEGE

The Academic Man
in the Catholic College

by John D. Donovan, *1918-*

SHEED AND WARD : NEW YORK

TO MY WIFE

PREFACE

This book is a sociological study of Catholic college professors. It is based, not on random observations and impressions, but on life-history data systematically collected during the Spring of 1960 in lengthy interviews with almost three hundred professors. Here they tell their stories, the stories of their family and educational backgrounds, their academic careers and work situations, their professional values and achievements, their satisfactions and their frustrations. And their stories, each in its own way, combine to outline and to describe the profile of the Catholic academic man.

The theoretical warrants for constructing this profile-in-depth of the Catholic college professor are many and important. Whether priest or layman, he is the central figure in the American Catholic Church's unique venture into the field of higher education. More than that, he is, by education and profession, an elite member of the Catholic community. What he is and thinks and does are conspicuous indices not only of the status but of the direction and speed of the social evolution of American Catholicism. Further, his professional role gives him the final responsibility of forming the minds and the hearts of the religious and lay persons who, as educated Catholics, are expected to constitute the leadership of tomorrow's generation.

These reasons for analyzing the situation of the Catholic professor did not, however, directly inspire the present study. Like most sociological surveys, it was conceived and born of more practical concerns. It was designed to provide at least a part of the empiric foundation necessary for a mature and critical evaluation of the state of American Catholic intellectual life.

As most informed Catholics and non-Catholics know, a sporadic but vigorous public debate has been carried on about this subject for almost a decade. The opening shot, so to speak, was fired by Msgr. John Tracy Ellis' report at a symposium of The Catholic Commission on Intellectual and Cultural Affairs. His socio-historical indictment of the quantity and quality of Catholic contributions to American intellectual life quickly provoked critical reactions. Almost immediately the debate was joined as Catholic intellectuals and professed non-intellectuals spoke and wrote their minds on both sides of the question. With the publication of Thomas O'Dea's trenchant analysis of the dilemma posed by the conflicting values of the intellectual life and of American Catholicism, a new and valuable focus was provided. As O'Dea pointed out, however, the arguments and rebuttals were necessarily short-sighted because of the paucity of empirically reliable data. The Catholic Commission on Intellectual and Cultural Affairs had reached a similar conclusion and at this point re-entered the picture. In order to provide an empiric foundation for these critical evaluations, they not only conducted their own questionnaire study of American Catholic intellectuals but they commissioned the present sociological survey.

The perimeters of the research reported here were in large part determined by practical considerations. The academic man, it is recognized, does not equal the Catholic intellectual community. He was selected for study, however, because, by any realistic yardstick, he and his fellows comprise the conspicuous majority of the Catholic intellectual elite. Admittedly, the exclusions of the faculty in Catholic women's colleges, and of Catholics on the staffs of non-Catholic colleges are significant research losses. But one can only speculate as to their consequences. Similarly, the absence of parallel data concerning the academic personnel of non-Catholic colleges severely limits the degree to which any evaluative comparisons can be made.

Our single focus, therefore, is the Catholic religious and lay professor in American Catholic coeducational and men's colleges and universities. Those whose life histories form the basis of our study were selected by statistically random procedures in order to maximize the probability of a representative cross-section. Inevitably, the statistical descriptions of their backgrounds and careers obscure the flesh-and-blood individuality of each professor and sacrifice the unique configuration of his life experiences to the composite profile of his colleagues. These costs, it is recognized, are not inconsiderable. Within their limits, however, there is solid reason to believe that the composite profile adequately and accurately describes the composition and the status of this segment of the Catholic intellectual community. The questionnaire and interview schedules used to collect the life-history data are not reproduced here. They are available on request from the author.

My indebtedness to so many persons for help and encouragement in this study very properly calls for acknowledgment. Foremost, I am grateful to Rev. William J. Rooney, the Executive Director of The Catholic Commission on Intellectual and Cultural Affairs. He was not only the moving force behind the decision to commission the survey, but he raised the necessary financial support and provided constant help and encouragement. In the face of both excusable and inexcusable delays in the completion of the study, he has been heroically patient and understanding. Second only to this initial debt, I am happy to express my thanks to the three hundred Catholic professors who followed up the generous co-operation of their presidents and accepted invitations to participate in the project. They were unfailingly courteous and kind, and their active interest and full co-operation were continuing sources of encouragement. In a very real sense it is their book.

I am also grateful to the administrative officers at Boston College for granting me a year's leave of absence from my teaching and administrative duties in order to design and carry out the research. Their generosity was only exceeded by that of my wife and children, who lived overlong with the research commitments of the academic man. In addition, Dr. John Van Tassel gave more of his time and talent than friendship could expect in helping to program and to process the data for computer analysis. I also had the advantage of receiving many helpful suggestions and constructive criticisms from Bernard Barber, Harry Johnson, Sister Marie Augusta Neale, S.N.D., C. Joseph Nuesse, Richard Robbins, and Robert G. Williams. I am grateful to all of these friends and associates. Like the CCICA, however, their association with the study in no way implies any endorsement of its design, facts, or interpretations. For these I alone take responsibility.

Finally, I am happy to acknowledge with gratitude the cheerful and competent clerical assistance provided at various times by Lorraine Bone, Elsa Dorfman, Aimée Noonan, Phyllis Pallett, Catherine Sullivan, and Mary Pat Schenk.

JOHN D. DONOVAN
Boston College

CONTENTS

Preface   *vii*

PART ONE: DESIGN AND PERSPECTIVES   3

  I THE SOCIOLOGY OF HIGHER EDUCATION   5
    Focus on the Faculty   5
    Where is the Catholic Intellectual?   6
    The Catholic Academic Man   7
    The Big Picture   10
    The Research Project: Design and Findings   11

  II PERSPECTIVES ON CATHOLIC HIGHER EDUCATION   15
  The Historic Structure of Catholic Higher Education   16
    Foundations and Survivals   17
    The Evolution of the Faculty   22
  The Religious Structure of Catholic Higher Education   25
    The Traditions of the Church   26
    Ecclesiastical Legislation   29
    The "Rule" and "Spirit" of the Congregation   33
    The Sub-Culture of American Catholicism   34
  The Dynamics of American Higher Education   36
    The Evolution of the University   37
    The Secularization Process   40
    Summary   44

PART TWO: SONS, STUDENTS, SCHOLARS   45

III THE SOCIAL ORIGINS OF THE FACULTY   47
   The Dimensions of Time and Space   48
      *The Age Structure of the Catholic College
         Faculty*   48
      *The Ecological Origins of the Catholic College
         Faculty*   50
   The Social Setting of the Family   51
      Parental Origins   51
      Parental Education   53
      Religious Affiliation   54
      Socio-Economic Status   55
   Parental Values and Influences   58
      Family Size and Birth Order   59
      The Structure of Parental and Familial Values 60
      *The Educational Values and Attitudes of the
         Parents*   64
      Summary   65

IV THE STUDENT LIFE OF THE ACADEMIC MAN   67
   The Pre-College Student Days   68
      Elementary School   68
      On to High School   73
   College and Seminary Days   75
   Graduate School   80
      Summary   85

V CLIMBING THE ACADEMIC LADDER   87
   Career Appointments and Career Mobility   88
      The First Rung of the Ladder   89
      —And There They Stayed   93
      Climbing the Ladder   95
   The Work Load of the Faculty   97
      Class Loads   98
      Non-Class Work Loads   99

Contents

Professional Symbols: Associations and Publications   *102*
  Associations and Conventions   *102*
  "Publish or Perish" ("or Parish")   *103*
The "Other" Factors: Church and Family   *105*
  Priest and Professor   *107*
  Family and Profession   *109*
  Summary   *110*

PART THREE: THE CATHOLIC PROFESSOR,
IMAGES AND REALITIES   *113*

VI PROFESSIONAL VALUES AND THEIR SOCIAL
  CORRELATES   *115*
Professional Values   *116*
  Teaching Satisfactions   *117*
  Role Preferences   *120*
  Value-Conflict Decisions   *124*
The Composite Value-Orientation Profile   *135*
Why?   *138*
  Professional Values and Family Socialization   *141*
  Professional Values and School Socialization   *146*
  Summary   *148*
VII THE PUBLISHING AND THE NON-PUBLISHING
  PROFESSORS   *151*
Facts and Assumptions   *152*
Publication and Family Socialization   *155*
  Family Environment   *155*
  Family Structures   *157*
Publication and School Socialization   *160*
  Pre-College Education   *162*
  College and University   *164*
  Summary   *167*
VIII SCHOLARSHIP AND THE INSTITUTIONAL SETTING   *169*
The Work Situation   *170*
  Policies and Practices   *170*

    Work Loads   175
    Supporting Services   177
  As the Faculty See It   180
    Satisfactions   181
    Frustrations   183
    Summary   184

PART FOUR: CATHOLIC HIGHER EDUCATION   187

  IX CONCLUSIONS   189
    The Facts   189
    The Problems   193
    The Projections   201
  APPENDIX: FACULTY PROFILES   207
  The Professional Scholars   207
    Rev. Bartholomew Anderson   207
    Dr. Arthur Buckley   209
  The Incomplete Academicians   212
    Rev. Daniel Catalano   212
    Dr. Charles Doherty   214
  The Uncommitted Teachers   216
    Rev. Francis Early   216
    Prof. Edward Flatley   217
Notes   221
Index   229

LIST OF TABLES AND FIGURES

Table 1 Statistical Profile of the Foundations, Administrative Controls, Closures and Life Tenures of Catholic Colleges for Men in the United States 20

Table 2 Levels of Educational Achievement of Parents of Catholic Academicians by Religious-Lay Status 53

Table 3 Occupations of Fathers of Catholic Academicians by Religious-Lay Status 56

Table 4 Type of Pre-College Education of Catholic Academicians by Religious-Lay Status (Percentages) 69

Table 5 Graduate Degree Attainments of Catholic Academicians and Other Academic Samples 82

Table 6 Degree Status of Catholic Academicians at First Faculty Appointment by Religious-Lay Status 90

Table 7 Distribution of Weekly Number of Credit Hours of Classroom Instruction of Catholic Academicians by Religious-Lay Status 98

Table 8 Distribution of Non-teaching Hours in Work Week of Catholic Academicians by Religious-Lay Status 99

Table 9 Work Load (Class and Laboratory Hours, Moderatorships, Committees, Student Conferences, etc.) for Week of Catholic Academic Man by Religious-Lay Status 101

Table 10 Publication Indices of Catholics Academicians and Lazarsfeld-Thielens Sample (Percentages)   *104*

Table 11 Distribution of Catholic Religious and Lay Academicians' Agreement and Disagreement with Statements of Major Teaching Satisfactions (Percentages)   *118*

Table 12 Distribution of Catholic Academicians by Rank Ordering of Role Preferences (Percentages)   *121*

Figure A Value-Orientation Sub-Profile of Catholic Academicians Based on Role Preferences (Percentages)   *123*

Table 13 Grand Summary Distribution of Catholic Religious and Lay Academicians by Conflict Decisions According to Hypothesized Research and Teaching Value-Orientations (Percentages)   *133*

Figure B Value-Orientation Sub-Profile of Catholic Academicians Based on Classification of Value-Conflict Decisions (Percentages)   *134*

Figure C Composite Value-Orientation Profile of Catholic Academicians Based on Role Preferences and Value-Conflict Decisions (Percentages)   *137*

Table 14 Distribution of Catholic Academicians' Value Orientations by Religious-Lay Status, Rank, Size of Institution, Academic Area and Publication Index (Percentages)   *139*

Table 15 Distribution of Catholic Academicians' Value Orientation by Education of Father and Occupation of Father (Percentages)   *142*

Table 16 Distribution of Catholic Academicians' Value Orientations by Father's Religion, Religious Climate of Family, Parental Authority, Parental Supervision, and Affective Ties to Parents (Percentages)   *143*

Table 17 Distribution of Catholic Academicians' Value Orientations by Type of School Attended at All Educational Levels (Percentages)   *147*

Table 18 Distribution of Catholic Academic Men in Publishing and Non-Publishing Samples According to Region of College, Size of College, Religious-Lay Status, and Subject Areas (Percentages) 153

Table 19 Proportions of Catholic Professors in Publishing and Non-Publishing Sub-groups by Catholic or Non-Catholic Institutional Sources of Bachelor's, Master's and Doctoral Degrees (Percentages) 165

Table 20 Institutional Sources of Satisfactions of Catholic Academicians by Religious-Lay Status (Frequency in Numbers) 181

Table 21 Institutional Sources of Frustrations of Catholic Academicians by Religious-Lay Status (Frequency in Numbers) 183

THE ACADEMIC MAN
IN THE CATHOLIC COLLEGE

PART ONE

DESIGN AND PERSPECTIVES

I

THE SOCIOLOGY OF HIGHER EDUCATION

During the past fifteen years national concern with the state of American intellectual life and with the problems of college and university education has been strikingly reflected in a rash of research activity in the behavioral sciences. For psychologists this involved merely a more extensive and a deeper cultivation of an established field of psychological investigation. For sociologists, however, it represented a new direction.[1] Indeed, with the notable exceptions of Veblen's critical evaluation of higher learning[2] and Wilson's analysis of the status of the academic man,[3] few significant sociological works had concentrated on the social structures and processes of higher education. As Caplow and McGee pointed out, "The methods of social research have been applied by university professors to every important American institution except their own."[4]

Focus on the Faculty

By way of acknowledging this professional myopia, a number of sociologists have recently turned their theoretical and research attention to the college and university scene and have contributed to the foundation of a sociology of higher education.

5

Typically, these studies have not attempted any Veblenian analysis of the social system of higher education but have empirically investigated specific sub-groups and processes. To the surprise of no one, the vulnerable and "captive" student group was promptly seized upon as a research laboratory and subjected to detailed study.[5] Only recently has the faculty member begun to receive the same attention.

For the most part the first empirical studies of the professional academician have dealt with specific problems: recruitment,[6] mobility,[7] the socio-political values of faculty members vis-à-vis academic freedom,[8] etc. In piecemeal fashion they have variously contributed to the construction of a social profile of the academic man and to the description of his professional culture. But the research gaps are still so numerous that only the dim outline of his professional role can yet be discerned.

Where is the Catholic Intellectual?

A clear, if somewhat parochial, illustration of these research gaps appears in the question posed vocally and frequently during recent years in American Catholic circles. Where is the Catholic intellectual? On the basis of recent sociological research it is known only that American Catholics are significantly underrepresented in the many Who's Who directories of intellectual leaders.[9] This is not a new finding, but it is one which has distressed an increasing number of articulate Catholic critics. With few dissents, the relative poverty of Catholic contributions to American intellectual life has been accepted as fact. The empirically unanswered sociological question is why.

In Catholic academic circles this question has stimulated a number of hypothetical explanations. Some, like Msgr. John Tracy Ellis, suggest that the impoverishment of Catholic intellectual life is related to the generally lower-class, non-intellectual traditions of the immigrant members of the Church and to the moral and practical orientations which have been conspicuous among ecclesiastical leaders and in educational objectives.[10] Others, such as Thomas O'Dea, have proposed that the paucity of Catholic intellectuals derives from, and reflects, the unique stamp of American Catholicism as a religious sub-system of the international Church.[11] In this view intellectual values and attitudes are inhibited in their development among American Catholics by religious structures and values which nurture formalism, clericalism, moralism, authoritarianism, and defensiveness.[12] Still other critics, such as Justus Lawler, express the view that the failure derives from a rejection of the theological and philosophical traditions which inspired Catholic intellectual life in earlier times.[13]

This sampling of analyses of American Catholic intellectual life does not, of course, do justice to the provocative lines of thought developed in them nor to the many shorter interpretations of other critics and apologists.[14] But it serves to identify a significant research gap in the sociology of higher education and to provide a raison d'être for the present study. Simply expressed, the basic purpose of this study is to contribute to the critical examination of Catholic intellectual life in the United States by providing for the first time a fund of empiric data describing the people who are formally identified as its foremost representatives.

The Catholic Academic Man

To begin with, the prevailing concept of "the Catholic intellectual" posed important and difficult problems. Depending on the definition, it could be enlarged or contracted at will. It could include artists, composers, critics, jurists, academicians, librarians

—all "whose main interest is the advancement of knowledge or the clarification of cultural issues and public problems."[15]

For the generally analytic purposes of Ellis, O'Dea, and others, the imprecision of this universe was tolerable. Their concern was more with the ideal type than with the concrete and specific varieties of intellectual roles. The logic as well as the logistics of empiric research, however, required that the universe be made specific and that a single intellectual role be isolated and defined for study. Here the research focus is on the Catholic academician, the full-time professional educator functioning at the college and university level.

Limiting the research universe to the Catholic academician finesses the problem of defining the intellectual but does not escape other potential sources of ambiguity. Technically, even this term would include a directory of persons so numerous and so varied (as to sex, ecclesiastical designation, institutional affiliation, etc.) as to compound the analytical as well as the procedural problems of research. As a necessary step, therefore, a sub-group of Catholic academicians had to be isolated for study. The Catholic academicians here studied are the men—the priests, brothers, and laymen—who are full-time members of the non-professional undergraduate and graduate schools' instructional staffs in Catholic coeducational and men's colleges and universities.[16]

This more precise specification of the research universe led to the exclusion, unfortunately, of other important sub-groups of Catholic academicians. Among these the most important are the faculties of American Catholic colleges for women and Catholic academicians on the staffs of non-Catholic institutions. The former group constituted, during the academic year 1958-59, 30% of the total full-time faculty in all American Catholic colleges—all told, some 3,410 professors, clearly a significant group in many respects. Their exclusion from the research universe of Catholic academic men does not, however, involve any great statistical loss, since only 17% of them were male.[17] The exclusion of Catholics on the staffs of non-Catholic colleges is, in this respect, a more significant loss. Not only are the majority of them men, but there appear to be *a priori* grounds for hypothesizing important differences in their backgrounds and professional roles as compared to their confreres in Catholic institutions. Numerically, of course, these professors constitute a smaller proportion of American Catholic academic men, and might have been included in the study. They were passed over only because there is no definitive register available to serve as a basis for a representative sampling.[18]

Other sub-groups excluded, but of lesser importance, were the faculties of professional schools—such as law, medicine, dentistry, social work, pharmacy, and nursing—college administrators, and part-time faculty. Except for the last named, these could be excluded without serious statistical loss: and their exclusion makes for greater homogeneity.[19] The part-time faculty members are, of course, important both in their increasing numbers (2,785 in 1958-59) and in their faculty roles. The split nature of these roles and the practical problems of their availability for interview were decisive in their exclusion from the study.

In short, the research universe here defined is limited to Catholic male religious and laymen who are full-time faculty members in undergraduate and graduate schools of Arts, Sciences, Business, and Education in Catholic coeducational and men's colleges. Statistically, this group comprised 7,847 faculty members, or 70% of the *total* faculty in such schools in Catholic higher education. Equally important is the fact that historically these faculty members have constituted the image of the academician in Catholic higher education for both Catholic and non-Catholic publics.

The rapid growth and development of Catholic women's colleges has in recent years added a new and important dimension to this image; but historical as well as logistical considerations have combined to restrict the scope of the survey to Catholic male academicians.

The Big Picture

In sociological perspective the Catholic academic man is a point of convergence for important theoretical and research interests in the sociologies of education, religion, and the professions. To these fields, as well as to the more vested interests of the Catholic community, the construction of a research-based profile of the Catholic academic man is an interesting and significant undertaking.

In its simplest form such a profile could sketch the lines which describe the career patterns and the professional values, attitudes, and behavior of the professors under study. These would be useful, of course; but limited to those dimensions, the profile would be so shallow and dimly lit as to be distorted. Only when perspective is supplied and when the skeletal structure of the personality-forming lines has been provided will such a profile emerge in depth and composition.

To this end the two chapters of Part One are directed. In the remaining pages of this chapter the rationale basic to the detailed structure of the study is outlined and the research design and major findings are summarized. Then, Chapter II provides a set of perspectives for viewing and interpreting the profile of the Catholic academic man by describing the major historical, socioreligious, and cultural factors relevant to his professional role and performance.

In Part Two the deeper, largely unseen, lines which structure the basic profile of the Catholic academic man are drawn by identifying the major socializing forces in his family and educational history. To this configuration, a surface is added by outlining the record of his academic career and by describing the professional environment in which he is now functioning.

In Part Three the professional visage provided by these personality-forming institutions is etched by identifying the professional values and attitudes which inform the role perception and role performance of the Catholic professor. Here, too, the differences in professional outlook and the patterns of socializing forces which produce them are distinguished. Chapters VII and VIII continue this analysis by describing the publishing and non-publishing professors, and the past and present factors significant to their status.

Finally, in Part Four the facts, problems and projections of Catholic higher education are described from the angle of vision of the faculty; and an attempt is made to define the present situation and to "predict" the situation of tomorrow.

The Research Project: Design and Findings

For the reader without leisure or without interest in technical details, this section summarizes the major features of the project design and of the research findings. It is necessarily brief and oversimplified, but it may help direct attention to areas of special interest which are more completely treated in the separate chapters and in the appendix.

The social profile of the Catholic academic man is the end product of detailed personal interviews with over three hundred religious and lay professors in twenty-two Catholic colleges and universities.[20] After substitutions and deletions, the sample comprised 267 Catholic college professors of whom 102 were religious and 165 lay persons. This number represented 87% of the projected sample. The random processes of choice provided 112 professors in the humanities, 98 in the social sciences, and 57 in the natural sciences. In terms of academic rank the sample was made up of 54 professors, 105 associate professors, 56 assistant professors and 50 instructors. In the absence of reliable information concerning the distribution of all Catholic college faculty members by subject area and rank, the representativeness of the sample in these respects can only be assumed. Independent critics have judged that the random sample drawn here is more rather than less representative of the research universe.

The research data were collected by questionnaire and interview, administered in each case by the author.[21] Each meeting took place on the particular campus and ranged in length from one and one-half to two and one-half hours. The questions were both directive and non-directive and were concerned with identifying biographical facts, values, interests, attitudes, etc., of the faculty member in his family and educational environments as well as in the present occupational setting. In almost every instance, favorable rapport was established between the interviewer and the respondents. The latter were interested in the research project and, as academic people, were sympathetic to the interviewer's efforts. As evidence of this, only one institutional substitution and fifteen faculty substitutions were required because of direct refusals to co-operate.

Before capsuling the research findings, one especially significant limitation of the research design and of the basis for interpreting the findings must be noted. This profile of the Catholic academic man cannot be projected against a comparably detailed sketch of his non-Catholic colleagues. The absence of such a control group makes impossible any direct comparison of Catholic and non-Catholic faculty members and handicaps any critical evaluation. Whenever possible, however, available research data descriptive of this larger academic group are presented so that some indirect comparisons can be made to the profile of the Catholic professor.

This research-based profile statistically describes the Catholic professor as the thirty- to forty-year-old son of predominantly urban-based, near-immigrant parents who were devout and life-long members of the Church. In the vast majority of cases, their parents had enjoyed few educational opportunities but had achieved some social mobility nonetheless. Typically, their fathers and mothers encouraged them in their educational aspirations, but with an eye to its practical rather than cultural values. They were quite strictly supervised during childhood and adolescence, and more often than not they felt closer to their mothers than to their fathers.

As students they were educated in Catholic institutions, at all levels, in far greater proportions than in non-Catholic schools. They were good students, but they were very conscious of strict supervision and the absence of intellectual challenges. As many describe it, they "went to school," they thought often and seriously about becoming priests, and many of the lay as well as the religious professors entered the seminary while still quite young. Those who persevered to ordination were usually assigned to their first collegiate position without the benefit of much extra-seminary graduate study. Their lay colleagues, on the other hand, joined the faculty in the greatest numbers after World War II in order to fill the staff needs created by the G.I. invasion. Too often, as they now testify, they accepted these appointments because they felt a need to serve the Church and because such positions were rewarding and prestigeful. Few had finished their graduate study at the time of their appointments, and the "unfinished thesis" still haunts the careers of many. On the job they have heavy work schedules, both in and out of class. They are teacher-scholars rather than research- and publication-minded scholars, and this is conspicuous in their professional values and in their poor records of publication. Their family and school socialization experiences are behind the differences in these values and publication records. Some are satisfied or only mildly frustrated with their present situation, but others are strongly disturbed by the persistence of many non-professional features in their work situations. This latter group are especially frustrated by their "second-class citizen" status and by the absence of institutional support for their career development. The vigor of these criticisms varies by institution and by individual professor. Some institutions, it may be expected, will lose some of their better lay staff members unless the changes underway are greatly speeded up. The majority will remain out of loyalty, out of personal satisfaction, out of professional concerns, or because they have nowhere else to go.

II

PERSPECTIVES ON CATHOLIC HIGHER EDUCATION

Like his professional colleagues in other institutions, the academic man in the Catholic college is formed in the crucible of many different environments. On the immediate and personal level, his basic personality and his orientation to social life are formed and developed by his family, his education, and his professional career. As so much psychological and sociological research has fruitfully established, his perception of his academic role and the patterning of his professional behavior have their roots in this early socialization. In large part, he is what he is because of what he learned and experienced as a child in a family, as a student in school, and as a member of an occupational group.

If the profile of the academic man is viewed only from this angle of vision, the perspective is so foreshortened that many professionally significant, broader forces are inevitably ignored. With the Catholic academician especially, such a narrow focus is particularly vulnerable to distortion. Like his non-Catholic colleague, he is heir to the history and the institutional dynamics of American higher education. Unlike them, he carries out his academic role within unique historical and ecclesiastical environments, those belonging to the religious sub-system of American Catholicism. As a background, therefore, to our profile, it will be necessary to sketch in the major relevant features of these environments. Proceeding from the more specific to the less so, we will briefly describe (1) the historical structure of American Catholic higher education, (2) the religious structure of the American Catholic Church, and (3) the institutional dynamics of American higher education.

THE HISTORIC STRUCTURE OF CATHOLIC
HIGHER EDUCATION

The unfortunate, but inescapable, first fact is that the definitive history of Catholic higher education in the United States has yet to be written. This observation does not demean or ignore the value of some historical research in this area, but it underscores its rarity.[1] Primary source materials, it is true, have been hard to acquire or have been of limited value; but it is clear that even these materials have been only partially exploited by Catholic educational historians, and have been ignored by the general historians of American higher education.[2]

With few exceptions, and some of these hardly noteworthy, the history of Catholic higher education in the United States can be learned only from the published "histories" of individual colleges. For the most part, these have been designed to serve local and special purposes and are historical only in a loose sense of the term. Some were obviously written to rekindle the memories and to sustain the pride of alumni or to commemorate in academic form a collegiate anniversary. Others had a more scholarly origin as graduate dissertations, but even these works are as a rule historically thin and superficial.[3] Typically, they honor the founding officers, describe the buildings, curriculum, and student body, and record by administrative periods the growth of the institution in terms of physical changes and enrollment statistics. For the most part, too, they are sympathetic chronicles rather than objective studies. Rarely do they provide the range and depth of detail that permit either a systematic analysis of institutional change or a comparative measure of the direction of the college's development. In fairness it must be recorded that the published history situation is but little better relative to the older and more numerous non-Catholic colleges and universities.[4]

More immediately significant is the fact that the available historical descriptions of Catholic higher education largely neglect the teaching staff. Except for the outstanding scholar and the traditional student favorite, the faculty is anonymous. Concerning the education of its members, their academic careers, their professional values, and their scholarly contributions, little or nothing is said. The paucity of reliable historical sources for such descriptions of the faculty must be acknowledged. The net result, however, is that the history of such a pre-eminently human process as education is largely dehumanized.

These historical gaps notwithstanding, a partial perspective for the interpretation of the profile of the Catholic academic man can be obtained by describing (a) the development of Catholic higher education in terms of institutional foundations, failures, and survivals; and (b) the major changes in faculty size and composition. As historical benchmarks these materials leave much to be desired, but they provide at least a minimal basis for that historical sensitivity so necessary for dynamic analysis and evaluation.

Foundations and Survivals

The history of Catholic higher education parallels in many respects the origins and development of other American colleges and universities. Like so many of these institutions, the first Catholic colleges were established originally as religious schools designed to provide pre-seminary and seminary education for prospective priests. Shortly thereafter, non-clerical students were enrolled in these colleges because, as Power points out, this primary motive for establishing the first colleges was reinforced by the needs "to create a center for missionary activities, and to provide a place where boys and young men might be given an opportunity to cultivate the moral virtues."[5]

The goal of intellectual development as a value in its own right was not unrecognized by the Catholic hierarchy, but the collegiate foundations which they initiated, sponsored, and encouraged were more immediately seen as concrete expressions of their apostolic and communal responsibilities. It was only in the late nineteenth century that the intellectual goals of Catholic higher education became more specific as a basis for collegiate foundations. The primary rationale remained religious and moral, but the significance of collegiate education for occupational and social mobility helped to enhance professional and academic values.

The chronology of these Catholic college foundations has been marked off by Power into three distinct periods, 1786-1849, 1850-1899, 1900 to date. The dating, of course, is only approximate, but it serves to distinguish what he describes respectively as the formative period, the period of development and experimentation, and the period of reorganization.[6] In each period significant changes are recorded in the definition of the functions of the college, in the curriculum and method, and in the internal organization of the program by general fields and departments. Like other church-related and secular colleges, but at a slower pace, Catholic colleges and universities became more professionalized and more academically mature.

Looked at in statistical form, the history of Catholic higher education during these periods pictures the high hopes, the frustrations, and the complex problems present to the growth of a collegiate educational system. Table 1 summarizes these growing pains by condensing Power's seventy-six-page appendix of historical sketches of each Catholic men's college in a statistical form.[7]

Except for Georgetown and St. Mary's College in Baltimore, all of the forty-two colleges established during the formative period were founded during the first half of the nineteenth century. As Table 1 indicates, the control of these early colleges was almost equally divided between the diocesan clergy and religious orders. It is clear, too, that almost all of the colleges experienced difficulties in establishing themselves, since 13 of the 30 which were finally closed lasted less than 10 years and another 12 colleges experienced changes in administrative control. The interesting fact is that the 12 which did survive this formative period survived, too, the competitive and other problems of the next 100 years and are still in existence. Regionally, slightly more than half as many colleges were established in the South as in the East and Midwest during this period. The mortality rates, however, show a reverse distribution, since only three of the Southern institutions have survived compared to five and six respectively in the East and Midwest.

During the second half of the nineteenth century the impact of the large-scale immigration of Catholics and of the changing social and economic situation is clearly reflected in the educational picture. In every region, but most notably in the South and Midwest, Catholic colleges were being hastily established and just as hastily closed. Within ten years, one-third of the 152 colleges established during this period had closed down and by the end of the century only 44 survived. It is significant to note

Table 1.—Statistical Profile of the Foundations, Administrative Controls, Closures, and Life Tenures of Catholic Colleges for Men in the United States*

Periods	No. of Colleges Founded	Types of Control					No. of Colleges Closed	Life Tenure (Yrs.) of Closed Colleges					
		Rel.	Dioc.	Lay	Unk.	Changes		1–10	11–20	21–30	31–50	51–99	Unk.
1786-1849	42	20	21	—	1	12	30	13	3	6	4	4	—
1850-1899	152	105	40	3	4	13	108	52	17	13	17	8	1
1900-1957	74	59	14	—	1	4	47	22	20	2	3	—	—
TOTALS	268	184	75	3	6	29	185	87	40	21	24	12	1

* Data compiled from Appendix A, Power, *op. cit.* Colleges surviving to 1957 include 12 founded between 1786 and 1849, 44 founded between 1850 and 1899, and 27 founded between 1900 and 1957. The total, 83 colleges, differs from the 101 Catholic coed and men's colleges reported in *The Official Directory, etc., 1959.* This may be accounted for by new colleges between 1957 and 1959 and by the new classification as coed of colleges which were once restricted to women.

that it was during this period that the religious orders of priests and brothers moved into the controlling position in Catholic higher education. An interesting aspect of this period, too, is the difference in the regional patterns of collegiate foundations and failures. In the East, despite the region's proportionately high Catholic population, it appears that colleges were established only when there were adequate provisions for their survival. Thus, of the 39 Catholic colleges established in that region between 1800 and 1899, only 20 eventually closed. This 51% failure figure seems high until it is realized that during the same period Catholic colleges for men established in the Midwest, South, and West were closed respectively in 66%, 87%, and 74% of the cases.

This historical chronicle of institutional instability was not, of course, unique to Catholic colleges. Hofstadter notes that Tewksbury "has found records of 516 colleges that were established before the Civil War in sixteen states of the Republic, and of these 104, or only 19 percent, survived!"[8] His data also indicate that among these non-Catholic institutions the rates of failure in the West and South were also clearly the highest.[9] During the post-Civil War period a considerably higher degree of stability was attained in both Catholic and non-Catholic institutions, but the incidence of institutional closings among the former still ran quite high.

In the twentieth century the most conspicuous feature of Catholic College development has been the rapid growth of women's colleges.[10] These institutions and their faculties are outside the range of the present study: but their increase during this period is interesting, not only because they are experiencing the usual financial and faculty problems of new colleges, but because they compete with Catholic male and coeducational institutions for the scanty resources and professional personnel available.[11] Ironically, their growth coincides with a sharp decline not only in the number of men's colleges established but in the latter's chances of survival. Thus, of the 74 men's colleges established between 1900 and 1957, 47 have already been closed. As in the previous period, the foundations attempted in the Midwest and in the South were considerably less successful in surviving than those colleges established in the East.

In summary it is clear that Catholic college education for men did not mature and achieve institutional stability until the last quarter-century. Throughout the greater part of the nineteenth century, well-intentioned but ill-advised diocesan and religious leaders confused the educational picture and subverted the establishment of a solid basis for collegiate development by founding too many colleges which were destined to an early demise. The record of 185 failures out of 268 colleges established is clear testimony to this.

The Evolution of the Faculty

To this record of institutional instability, another dimension of the historical background of the Catholic academic man is provided by describing the evolution of the faculty to which he now belongs. For the definition of his professional role, the patterns traced by his predecessors in Catholic higher education constitute both a point of reference and an occupational environment. The traditions which they established and the professional values which they recognized are important for his contemporary situation of action.

Throughout most of the nineteenth century, the evolution of the Catholic college faculty parallels the historical situation in other American colleges. Typically, the first faculty members were priests assigned to the newly established colleges by their religious or diocesan superiors. Many of them were foreign-born

Europeans who had been educated abroad prior to their mission assignment to the United States. With few exceptions both they and their native-born clerical colleagues were the products of a seminary education which was more vocational than intellectual in its orientation.[12] Indeed, the faculty shortage throughout this period was so acute that seminarians were often pressed into service as teachers two or three years before completing their theological studies.[13] Catholic educational historians provide practically no information concerning the academic credentials of this clerical faculty in either degree or scholarship terms. Some outstanding intellectual figures have, of course, been identified, but they appear to have been exceptions to the general pattern of professional mediocrity. In justice, of course, it must be recalled that these were the pioneer, "mission" days of the Catholic Church in the United States.[14] The luxury of time for the development of professional competence was seldom available to the priest-professor of the early collegiate foundations.

The lay members of the Catholic college faculty during the nineteenth century are almost unknown to us. Some were refugee scholars from Europe, others were ex-seminarians recruited to college teaching because they were safe and inexpensive.[15] Numerically they were never a significant group during this period, since they were appointed only when the necessary number of clerical professors could not be provided. In 1850, for example, they numbered only 26 out of a faculty of 240 in 25 colleges.[16] This proportion increased so slowly that by 1872 in 55 colleges with a total faculty of 677,597 were male religious and only 80 were laymen.[17] In American higher education during the post-Civil War period this clear-cut domination of the teaching staff by priests and brothers was a significant point of contrast to the situation in other American colleges. Initially they, too, had been staffed largely by clergymen, but after 1860, despite a continuance of denominational control, the faculty was composed increasingly of lay professors. Moreover, in at least the major institutions, many of these non-Catholic faculty members were the holders of advanced graduate degrees and were oriented in the new university structure to productive research as an integral part of their professional roles.[18] The Catholic faculty, still predominantly clerical, had few professors with advanced degrees in any but the sacred sciences and was still preoccupied with the teaching function as the exclusive component of its professional role.

Against this background the changes in the composition and qualifications of the Catholic college faculty during the present century are revolutionary. Slowly at first, but with increasing frequency since 1930, the Catholic college scene has been marked by the invasion of the lay faculty members. In 1924 they numbered only 1,859 and constituted 56% of the teaching staff. By 1934, ten years later, they made up 62% of the faculty.[19] This proportion changed only slowly until the end of World War II, but then the gates were forced open by the pressure of student enrollments. At the moment, in Catholic colleges for men, laymen are approaching 70% of the teaching staff.[20]

During the first decades of this century, only a few of the lay professors recruited to teach in Catholic colleges had advanced degrees or an interest in scholarly work. Some were ex-seminarians, others were honor graduates of previous classes, still others were teachers in Catholic secondary schools. Gradually, however, this recruitment pattern changed as Catholic universities were established and as religious superiors sent young priests to non-Catholic as well as Catholic graduate institutions to acquire advanced degrees.

Since World War II the composition and qualifications of Catholic faculty members have changed rapidly and radically, altering the collective profile. This fact, with its implications, has been only partly recognized within Catholic circles, and even less in non-Catholic academic groups.[21] In their details these topics will concern us later. Here, in the interests of critical perspective, it is only important to indicate that the Catholic academic man of today is a new species. He is a layman more often than a priest. He is professionally rather than spiritually oriented to his career. But he is, whether priest or layman, newly arrived on the scene, and he does not yet dominate the faculty profile. The shadow of his predecessors—some are still his colleagues—is still conspicuous. So he works within an environment only partially adapted to the new values and new perspectives which he brings to the academic life.

THE RELIGIOUS STRUCTURE OF CATHOLIC
HIGHER EDUCATION

No less important than the perspective provided by the history of Catholic higher education is the perspective provided by its specifically religious organizational structure. In one form or another, such a religious background is a part of the occupational environment of all academic persons in the United States. The case of the Catholic academic man is unique not only in the persistence of the ecclesiastical environment but in the specific structure of religious authority. In the United States, Catholic colleges are extensions of the Church established and directed by religious authorities in order to fulfill its traditionally defined teaching mission.

Historically, the formation and administration of such institutions at this educational level is a unique role for Catholic priests and ecclesiastics. Indeed, as Fr. Walter Ong, S.J., points out, "American Catholic universities and colleges represent a direct large-scale venture into higher education such as the Catholic Church has never attempted in the past or elsewhere in the present."[22] The uniqueness and the reasons for this venture will not concern us here. The point is that the ecclesiastical establishment and administration of American Catholic colleges and universities "involve" the Catholic academic man in an environment composed of at least the following significant variables: (a) the tradition of the Church; (b) ecclesiastical regulation; (c) the "rules" of specific religious societies and congregations; (d) the cultural variants of all these dimensions developed historically within American Catholicism. The complexities of each of these variables and the institutionalized differences in their meaning for the Catholic academic man (for example, the different significance of canon law and the "rule" of a religious congregation for a priest-professor and for a layman) preclude any detailed discussion of their functional importance. It will only be possible to sketch selectively some of the direct and indirect implications of this complex religious structure for the professional role and career of the academic man.

The Traditions of the Church

Unlike his colleagues in non-Catholic institutions, the Catholic academic man lives his professional life within the framework of a religious structure in which a many-sided tradition of centuries informs substantial portions of his thought and activity. Here, of course, the concept of "tradition" must be understood in both the special theological meaning it has in Catholic thought and in its more general cultural sense as an historic deposit of values, beliefs, and attitudes. At both levels the tradition of the Church contributes elements important not only to religious and intellectual socialization but to the professional environment.

The complexities of the theological concept of tradition need not detain us. Basically, it includes not only the revealed truths of sacred Scripture but the *unwritten* revelations which have been interpreted and transmitted by the Church.[23] Operationally it is this religious tradition expressed as theological and philosophical values and beliefs that undergirds the Catholic academic man's self-concept and life orientation. He believes, for example, that man is made in the image and likeness of God; that the Incarnation changed man's fate and made Heaven his destination; that the supernatural order is real and supra-scientific and superior to the natural order; that the Church instituted by Christ speaks with infallible authority in matters of divine truth and doctrine and with a defined authority in matters peripheral to doctrine. Moreover, on other, less theological levels the Catholic academic man has been socialized in traditions derived partly from ecclesiastical and partly from historical-cultural sources. Thus, he is conditioned to think in terms of the absolute, to act on the level of principle, and to prefer the deductive over the inductive. If he is a priest, he enjoys privileges and he acquires responsibilities which have tradition as well as law at their source. If he is a layman, he shares in a different way in the priesthood of Christ and has rights and duties not only theologically defined but culturally conditioned.[24] To the degree that the Catholic academic man has been exposed to and has accepted this religious tradition, he is a tradition-directed man—but in a sense far more profound and positive than the pale and passive prototype that David Riesman constructed in *The Lonely Crowd*.[25] His religious socialization has committed him to an active frame of reference. The impact of this on his self-concept and his role-concept will, of course, vary from person to person. For every academic man, however, this religious tradition is a significant fact of orientation. Moreover, it is an orientation made inescapable, if not reinforced, by the religious spirit and climate of the Catholic campus.

At a more immediate and academic level, the Catholic professor functions within the context of other traditions which are now relatively unique in the American educational scene. These traditions of mixed religious and historical ancestry include an explicit preference for the separate education of the sexes, the historical bias in favor of humanistic studies, the omnibus leadership of the clergy, etc. Considerations other than tradition are needed to explain these policies. But, the critical point here is that they are perceived *as* traditions and supported by the Church's bureaucratic bias to the rule of the elders, and that they block or slow down any significant change. Thus, despite the shortage of Catholic professors and other resources and despite the pattern provided by other American colleges and universities, tradition still recommends, where it does not require, the separate education of boys and girls at the college level. There are some recent exceptions to this tradition, but the general pattern remains one of colleges for boys administered by priests and brothers and separate colleges for girls administered by teaching nuns. Often they are physically adjacent to one another, but for many complex reasons there are still no parallels to the academic interchanges of Harvard-Radcliffe, Brown-Pembroke, Columbia-Barnard, etc.

Similarly, Church legislation as well as tradition has perpetuated the pattern of clerical leadership within the limitations of a provincial or regional structure and despite the numerical majority of the lay faculty member. Thus, not only is the president of the Catholic college almost always a religious but he is a religious selected for the position from the limited numbers, or cadre, of religious within the province or diocese.[26] In most other American colleges and universities there is no such traditional or legislative restriction on the choice of leaders.[27]

Clearly, the foregoing examples of religious tradition as it appears in Catholic higher education are selective and incomplete. They serve only to establish the fact that the Catholic academic man is "involved" in traditions which importantly condition his perception of his professional role and which permeate his institutional setting.

Ecclesiastical Legislation

The canon law of the Church provides still another unique and significant element in this professional environment. These codes are more frequently and more directly pertinent to the religious members of the faculty, but they affect, too, directly or indirectly, the work situation of the layman.

The most universal and direct injunction relative to their intellectual activity is provided by the Index of Forbidden Books. Typically, permission to read such books is readily provided by religious authorities for both the faculty members and their students. Nonetheless, the very existence of such a code and the slight inconvenience which the necessary permission requires are nuisance factors which "get in the way" of intellectual activity. Moreover, most Catholic academic men are disturbed because many of their non-Catholic colleagues regard the Index as an instrument of repression exercised by a monolithic Church to deny scholars the intellectual freedom which the pursuit of truth requires. This imputation has little contemporary basis in fact, but for the Catholic academic man the Index remains an embarrassing bit of ecclesiastical legislation.[28]

For the religious members of the Catholic college faculty and for the religious administrators, the legislation of the Church has more direct relevance. Its prohibition against "vagrant" priests and religious requires that every religious member of the faculty be formally and specifically under the jurisdiction of a bishop or religious superior. The implications of this requirement are both extensive and profound. By vow or solemn promise each priest and religious is bound by obedience to accept the assignments of his superiors. Whether he teaches, what he teaches, where he teaches, when he teaches, all are decisions removed from his personal control and reserved for his religious superiors. In practice, of course, the rigidity of this situation is often softened by active consideration of the priest's or brother's personal and academic qualities and preferences. Moreover, he is not only permitted but encouraged to express his preferences to his superiors. But in the last resort, the primary considerations are not the personal preferences of the religious member of the faculty but the broader interests or needs of the congregation and his own spiritual growth and development. The priest-professor in the Catholic college is not and cannot be a free professional in the academic market place.

It should be pointed out that while the religious faculty member in the Catholic college is not a free professional, his dual role as priest and professor does not inevitably and inherently result in conflicting role expectations. Within the ideal construct of the priesthood as a total status, the professional obligations of his academic role can be integrated with those of his priesthood and can be perceived as his unique and priestly contribution to the care of souls and to the reconstruction of the world in Christ.[29] In the experience of the Church such an ideal integration of the religious and the academic roles is the uncommon situation. Therefore, in order to protect the higher-valued role of the priest, ecclesiastical law reserves to the religious superior of the priest-professor the right to set the perimeters of his academic role.

Regarding the administration of Catholic colleges and universities, there are other relevant and significant Church laws.

The most important of these limits the tenure of the *religious superior* of a congregation to two successive three-year terms of office, or a total of six years. Since the offices of president of the college and religious superior have generally been held conjointly, a new chief administrative officer of the college has been appointed every six years, if not oftener. As Riesman and Jencks have observed, the faculty members have been more permanent than the administrators and from their entrenched position could often effectively resist the "itinerant Administration."[30] If, as a latent function, this short-tenure policy gives the faculty a negative type of power, it also inhibits the prospects of long-range planning and policy continuity essential to institutional development. On occasion this canonical requirement serves to relieve a college of an ineffective administrator, but since the appointive powers are held by higher-echelon superiors (provincials and bishops) who are removed from the college, limited in their own tenure, and responsible for the broader functions of the congregation, the process is vulnerable to influences and considerations that are non-academic and non-professional. In point of fact, the provincials and bishops are selected on the basis of qualities other than intellectual and frequently have little or no experience with institutions of higher learning.[31]

There can be little question but that these ecclesiastical regulations and policies significantly affect the institutional environment of a Catholic college. The clerical members of the faculty, of course, are the most exposed and the vulnerable group. The president of the college is not only their academic superior, but he may also be the immediate, responsible authority for their religious lives. Toward him they must play dual roles and manifest dual loyalties. These roles are not necessarily in conflict with one another, but the conditions for conflict are clearly present. The priest-professor is exposed to pressures that the lay-professor does not experience. On occasion this may lead him to subordinate his loyalty to his scholastic discipline in favor of loyalties institutionalized for him as a member of a religious community and as a subject of a religious superior. Compared to the layman, the priest-professor is not free to press without ambivalence the professional demands of his academic role. In addition, as a religious, he has no professional right to expect institutional tenure. The number and types of positions to which he may be assigned are limited by the functions of his community within a province or district, but each year he must wait, hopefully or fearfully, for the publication of assignments from the provincial superior.

The lay members of the faculty are not, of course, subject to the authority of these religious superiors. At the same time this religiously-oriented occupational climate is not without its significance for their academic life. The omnipresent symbols of religious authority, the emphasis upon institutional loyalty, the different kind of role relationship which they and their religious colleagues have to the administration are all conspicuous facts. On matters of institutional policy and practice, for example, they inhibit free and open communication between the religious and lay members of the faculty. In some instances, lay members are expected to concur, uncritically, with the decisions which religious members are *required to accept—accept, that is, without, at least, public demurrer.* As a free professional the lay academician in the Catholic college cannot be silenced, but his vigorous and outspoken objections, before and after administrative decisions, are sometimes viewed as disloyalty according to the authority-obedience value structure of the religiously-oriented culture.

The impact of ecclesiastical regulations and the occupational environment which they help to establish differs by individual faculty member, by institution, and even by the religious order or congregation administering the college: but the critical fact is that the institutional environment *is* affected, significantly and pervasively, by Catholic ecclesiastical law and by the occupational culture which it tends to create. In American higher education it is a unique institutional setting, and it must be taken into account in any critical evaluation or interpretation of the values, attitudes, and behavior of the Catholic academic man.

The "Rule" and "Spirit" of the Congregation

At a still more specific level, the professional environment is influenced by the "rule" and "spirit" of the religious society or congregation in administrative charge. The Jesuits, Dominicans, Benedictines, and the other orders and congregations all share the traditions of the Church and are equally subject to its canonical codes. Each group, however, has a distinctive religious personality and a concept of education which are venerated, codified, and expressed in a distinctive "spirit" or life orientation. The religious members of the faculty learn this rule and spirit in their seminary days and are expected to live according to its dictates as priests and professors.

In each order and congregation, a minimal feature of the rule is the time-consuming round of spiritual exercises which each religious must perform. Mass, meditation, spiritual reading, Vespers, etc.—these and other obligations are combined in different forms in the rule of each congregation. In addition each has its own specific rules and its own hierarchy of virtues and, by extension, these are associated with the colleges it administers. In Catholic circles especially, the stereotypes induced by these rules are well known. The Jesuits, for example, are often identified as sophisticated dialecticians, the Dominicans as philosophic systematizers, the Benedictines as spiritual stabilizers, etc. The accuracy of these oversimple identifications is not relevant here. The more important fact is that the values and emphasis structured in an order's rule and spirit are reflected in the objectives, the curriculum, and the academic style of its colleges. The classic illustration here, of course, is the Jesuit *Ratio Studiorum,* but similar, if less formal, models are still present in other academic traditions. Time and accommodation to the American scene have all but demolished the detailed relevance of models like the *Ratio* to the contemporary scene in Catholic higher education. But the spirit of Jesuit or Dominican or Benedictine life still distinguishes the environment of its college. The sub-culture of each religious congregation marks its educational institutions with the stamp of its unique personality.

For the lay faculty member, the rule and the spirit of the religious group in charge are structural and situational facts of importance. He is not obligated to any part of the rule, nor is he expected to accept or internalize the spirit. At the same time it is impossible for him to be indifferent to the official as well as the informal expressions and manifestations of these distinctive religious values and attitudes. Administrative policy reflects them, the religious members of the faculty live them, the curriculum often expresses them; even the students or their parents may expect and emphasize them.

The Sub-Culture of American Catholicism

Finally, and briefly, the background of the Catholic academic man is filled with the lights and shadows provided by the cultural accommodation of the Church to the American scene. The product of this accommodation is the distinctive and complex sub-culture of American Catholicism. Catholics and non-Catholics alike "know" that as a socio-religious system it differs from the Catholicism of Germany, Spain, France, etc. The differences, however, spring from so many sources and find so many expressions that a simple characterization is difficult and dangerous.

Basically, American Catholicism is the Church grounded in the unity of divine revelation, theology, and ecclesiastical law, but adapted historically and culturally to the dynamic features of the American way of life and to the ethnic, economic, and social composition of its members. Within the broad limits of variation open to its cultural form, it reflects these forces in varying degrees. It is near-immigrant, working-class, Democratic, activist, pragmatic, self-conscious as a minority, and powerful. It is authoritarian in a democratic society, militantly theistic in a secular culture, and tradition-centered in an other-directed value system. In image and in fact it is many other things, too, for Catholics and non-Catholics alike. The central fact is that American Catholicism is a distinctive socio-religious sub-system which expresses the accommodation of religious values and organization to the American environment.

The immediate point is that this American Catholic sub-culture constitutes a frame of reference for the academic life and activity of the Catholic professor. Thus, the "traditions" of the European past, the injunctions of ecclesiastical law, and the "rule" and "spirit" of religious congregations have taken on new dimensions as they meet the American scene and the American Catholic community. The basic values and orientations have not been set aside, but they have been adapted to new needs and new situations. This process has not been unresisted within the Church and within the American Catholic population, but it has taken place. Thus, the separate education of the sexes in Catholic schools and colleges has been yielding to the pressure of numbers and to the model of non-Catholic coeducation. Similarly, the authority of the clergy is perceived in more functionally specific terms, the knowledge of empiric science and the values of the inductive approach are more positively accepted, and the secular is less frequently identified as inevitably anti-religious.

More specifically, the educationally relevant codes of ecclesiastical law have been accommodated to the larger cultural situation. The process is uneven and incomplete, and this in itself affects the professional life of the Catholic professor. The Index is a continuing fact, but its restrictive spirit has been eased and its ecclesiastical red tape has been cut. Similarly, the canon-law-based problem of continuity in the religious leadership of Catholic colleges has been finessed by separating the offices of religious superior and institution president. Even the ecclesiastical authority of the hierarchy and of religious superiors has been conditioned by the culturally dominant anti-authoritarian values and by the pressures to democracy of accrediting and other professional associations.

The same picture of accommodation appears in the "rule" and "spirit" of religious congregations. Some of the more rigorous requirements have been relaxed so that the priests and brothers have a mobility and range of freedom relatively unknown in earlier periods. The sacrosanct curriculum and institutional styles have been set aside or preserved only in part. In many other direct and subtle forms this intra-religious accommodation has found expression. The Jesuits, Benedictines, etc., are still recognizably similar to their religious confreres around the world, but within the international congregation the American Jesuit, for example, is a distinct socio-religious personality type.

THE DYNAMICS OF AMERICAN HIGHER EDUCATION

In addition to the influence of these unique historical and religious environments, the Catholic academic man's professional situation is affected by his exposure and relationship to the broader institutional dynamics of American higher education. These forces and currents are far too numerous and complex for detailed analysis. Two directions of institutional development in American higher education are so directly and pervasively relevant, however, that an adequate critical perspective requires their separate treatment. Specifically, it is important to interpret the situation of the Catholic academic man with reference to (a) the evolution of the university, and (b) the process of secularization.

The Evolution of the University

There is little doubt but that in contemporary American educational circles the university is the measure and the model of intellectual leadership. Harvard, Columbia, Princeton, Yale, Chicago, California, etc., are identified as the centers of intellectual progress. Each began as a college concerned primarily with undergraduate instruction. Each still has a college or many colleges as its basic unit. But at Harvard, Columbia, and most of the others, it is not the college but the university which looms large. The professional and graduate schools have in numbers and spirit dominated the collegiate image and have transformed the traditional values associated with the role and functions of the faculty.

Historically this evolution of the university and of the academic role are phenomena only a century old. Prior to the Civil War, the conservation of knowledge was viewed as the major academic function, and the almost exclusive role of the professor was that of instruction. Metzger describes the evolution of the university in the following words:

By 1860 the signs were pointing to a drastic revision of the goals of the college system. The growing emphasis on scholarship, the questioning of old pedagogical assumptions, the enlarging scale of philan-thropy, were converting the larger colleges into institutions geared for research. At the same time, as the result of deeper social forces at work, the "conserving" function of the college no longer loomed so large. The unhinging of moral certainties by urban living, the fading out of the evangelical impulse, the depersonalization of human rela-tions in the process of industrial expansion, were destroying that inte-gral vision, that firm and assertive credulity, required of institutions devoted to conservation. Two other forces were to consummate this shift from "conserving" to "searching" in the universities of postwar America. The first was to be the powerful impact of Darwinism, which would unlock the creative potential of the American academic science. The second was to be the influence of the German university, whose scholarly lore and academic traditions Americans admired and adapted. By 1860, the American colleges stood at the verge of a new outlook; two or three decades later, they would possess it fully.[32]

Catholic higher education was until recent years outside the range of these university molding influences. As Power has pointed out:

During the period in the United States when university foundations were being laid, Catholic colleges acted as if science and research did not exist. This isolationist attitude, coupled with the colleges' preoccu-pations with the past, worked to the disadvantage of their graduates and helped to keep them from a place of influence in forming Ameri-can ideals. . . . From all that was written during the years a Catholic university for America was being discussed, it seems apparent that few Catholics had any clear idea of what a university was.[33]

In the light of the social and economic condition of American Catholics, it is not surprising that the university idea developed only slowly and against much resistance. For more than half a century Catholic higher education was outside the involvement which sparked the evolution of the university and which broadened the features of the academic role. Typically, the institutional objectives and the training of the faculty emphasized moral education and the conservation of knowledge. They had little contact with, and little sympathy for, the German-inspired model of the university's function in creating new knowledge by faculty research and publication. The "good" professor was one who knew the traditional knowledge of his field and was effective in communicating it to his students. An interesting sidelight, too, was the high value placed upon rhetorical and debating skills. The Catholic professor of this era was expected to defend the traditional truths and to view critically the "new" knowledge. There was, of course, neither the disposition nor the time nor the background-training for research.

During the past thirty years, the university model of higher education and the institutionalization of faculty research and publication have increasingly found acceptance in Catholic circles. The "cultural lag" of Catholic higher education in these respects has been reduced but is still manifest. In some administrative circles there exists a deep-seated ambivalence toward what appear to be the irreconcilable functions of teaching and research as proper functions of the faculty member. A large number of the religious and lay members of the faculty share this ambivalence and tend to reject the research-publication function. For the most part they are products not only of Catholic elementary and secondary school education but Catholic college and graduate programs. In their generation as students, the emphasis on conserving and transmitting knowledge as well as the teacher models to which they were exposed provided little basis for positive acceptance of the university ideal and of the academician's responsibilities for research and publication.

Resistance to the definition of research and publication as a proper function of the faculty is not, of course, unique to Catho-

lic higher education. But it is significant not only as a characteristic of the system of American Catholic higher education but
also as a factor important to a critical evaluation of the professional performance of the Catholic academic man.

The Secularization Process

With the development of the university during the latter part
of the nineteenth century American higher education began a
process in which secular values were substituted for those of a
religious cast. Symbolically this process was marked by the
defrocking of those who sat in the president's chair; more important, however, was the systematic scientific attack on the
theological premises and moral orientation of earlier American
higher education.[34]

The historical reasons why American higher education became
secularized are many and complex. The scepticism of the scientific mind, the growing importance of the secular professions,
the increasing importance of the voice of business in the academy, these and other forces weakened the position of the religious orientation and of denominational control. The fact, as
Parsons expresses it, is that

> . . . whatever the social mechanisms involved, the American system of
> higher education in both its publicly supported colleges and universi-
> ties (state and municipal) and its private sector is now firmly secular
> in its major orientation. The sole major exception is the educational
> system controlled by the Catholic Church, though there are smaller-
> scale ones for Lutherans, Jews, etc. The Catholic is a large minority,
> but there seems to be no basis for believing that its pattern can serve
> as a model for the reversal of this fundamental trend, if indeed the
> Catholic educational pattern can itself survive for very long against
> the trend.[35]

As the sole major exception to the secularization process, the Catholic system of higher education is not only unique on the American scene but it is inevitably involved either in the defense of its philosophy of higher education or in the piecemeal accommodation of its system to the dominant and competitive models of non-Catholic colleges and universities. The intellectual world, as well as the paying public, uses the philosophy, the curriculum, and the faculty of such institutions as Harvard, Chicago, California, etc., as its yardsticks. With few exceptions, Catholic educators also respect the intellectual quality of these leading universities, but their own theological, philosophical, and ecclesiastical commitments permit them to follow the secular pattern to only a limited degree.

These resistant and adaptive reactions of Catholic educators to the secularization process are neither unusual nor surprising. During the latter part of the nineteenth century, Protestant denominations fought the same losing battle. At that time, the relatively small size of the Catholic collegiate system and the more general isolation of the Catholic community from the life of the society served to forestall the problem and the pressure for its resolution. But then as now the problem of secularization was posed in many forms and was being met by many different types of accommodation.

In Catholic circles the secularization of knowledge is often equated with the more comprehensive philosophy of secularism or scientific humanism. Viewed in this fashion it is identified as anti-religious rather than non-religious in its definition of man and society. As so many recent Papal encyclicals have indicated, such a view of man's nature and destiny contradicts the Catholic concept of man's supernatural attributes and transcendental end. The natural order is not denied a positive value in this Catholic perspective, but its description as a secondary good has his-

torically led to a demeaning of the world and of natural knowledge. American Catholics have been particularly vulnerable to
this distorted interpretation of the natural order, which, in part
at least, explains the resistance of Catholic educational leaders
to the process of secularization. More recently, this view of the
secular has been modified and its right to recognition as, precisely, secular and thus outside the sphere of religious interest
has been acknowledged.[36] This has permitted an attention to
empiric science and a respect for scientific truth not previously
possible. By definition, however, the Catholic measure of primary
reference is related to the supernatural and moral good which is
man's primary goal. In a faculty composed of both religious and
lay members, this means that the problem of properly ordering
the sacred and the secular inevitably produces tension. Education, viewed as moral and as conserving, sought and still seeks
an acceptable pattern of accommodation to the more secular
climate of the dominant educational scene. Theology as a science
rather than an apologetic, the behavioral sciences as independ-
ently valuable rather than as "proofs" of social philosophy, philosophy as a discipline rather than as an ideology, these and other
developments illustrate the attempts of Catholic higher education to achieve a dynamic equilibrium in which the sacred and
the secular are each accorded a respected place. So far the
equilibrium has not been attained—if indeed it can be without
major institutional changes.

A special and unique aspect of the process of secularization in
Catholic colleges concerns the administrative offices. These have
been, and are, almost automatically reserved for the religious.
Indeed, the defrocking of the incumbent of the president's chair
and the installation of a layman as president appears to be a
remote prospect.[37] The authoritarian structure of the Church and
the ecclesiastical as well as theological ordering of the religious

and lay statuses are fundamental blocks to the abdication of clerical authority and responsibility. Under pressure, lay members of the faculty have been appointed to the office of dean and vice-president, but in the structure of the Catholic university their authority seldom is equal to their responsibility and they serve without administrative tenure at the will of the religious president and the religious board of trustees. The pressure toward increased participation of the faculty, religious and lay, in the formation of university policy has been a recent phenomenon in Catholic higher education. It is such a new pressure, and one for which the structure of religious life has so ill prepared administrators, that some overt tensions have developed. As a result of increased pressure from the lay and some religious members of the faculty—often in the form of an AAUP chapter—there have been more and more concessions to the voice of the faculty. The process of secularization has gone no farther in this respect, but in this as well as other areas the process of accommodation predicted by Parsons appears to be well underway. Indeed, the process of accommodation between the religious administration and the lay members of the faculty in a Catholic college may prevision the new form of religious-lay relationship which, as the ecumenical councils reflect, must be institutionalized in order to avoid the growth of anticlericalism and in order to re-establish the layman's proper role in the theology of the Church.[38]

This broader question is here only indirectly relevant. The process of secularization in Catholic higher education is in microcosm the process and the problem of the Church. Lay representation and lay or secular values in higher education no less than in the Church are pressing for recognition. The Catholic college, still only partially and reluctantly open to the secularization process, is an ideological battleground. And this battleground, with its opposing strains and pressures, is the setting in which the Catholic academic man works. Compared to the academicians in most non-Catholic American colleges, the "damned if you do and damned if you don't" environment is not only a unique academic setting but one that must be appreciated in any critical evaluation of the Catholic academic man's role and performance.

Summary

The premise of this chapter was that the academic man in the Catholic college could only be properly described and analyzed against the background of his occupational environment. Specifically, the relatively recent achievement of institutional stability in Catholic higher education and the even more recent domination of the faculty by lay persons are historical facts too often ignored or minimized. Further, the impact of the religious structure of Catholic academic life in the form of religious tradition, canon law, and the "rule" of specific congregations were all seen as unique and significant environmental factors. Finally, against the background of the institutional dynamics of American higher education, the cultural lag of Catholics in accepting the model of the university and their resistance or reluctant accommodation to the secularization process have, in time and in spirit, placed special features in the framework for the evaluation of the role of the Catholic academician.

PART TWO

SONS, STUDENTS, SCHOLARS

III

THE SOCIAL ORIGINS OF THE FACULTY

The decision to begin the biographical profile of the Catholic academic man by describing his social origins follows a pattern common to similar psychological and sociological studies.[1] The underlying hypothesis is that the values, attitudes, and patterns of behavior learned as a child in a family form a basic personality structure which is expressed in individual motivations and role perceptions as an adult.

To test this hypothesis alongside the Catholic academic man requires detailed information concerning the latter's professional life, but it requires first the critical description and analysis of these early socializing influences. How old is he? Where was he born? Who were his parents and grandparents? In what kind of family setting did he grow up? What were the values, attitudes, and patterns of behavior taught or exemplified by his mother and father? These and other questions probe the sources and the types of influence which have conditioned the evolution of his life orientation and work culture. In individual cases one or another source and type of influence may be especially important, but the present concern is with the patterns or configurations of socializing forces which may distinguish the sample of Catholic academicians as a whole. In outline form and without distinguishing between the clerical and lay members of the Catholic college faculty,[2] these socializing forces will be described in terms of (a) the dimensions of time and space, (b) the social setting of the professor's family of orientation, and (c) the structure and content of parental values and influences.

THE DIMENSIONS OF TIME AND SPACE

Even before he was born, the Catholic academic man, like all men, was destined to be influenced by general and impersonal forces over which he had no control. Thus, he was at once conditioned in the content and form of his early socialization by the specifics of the time of his birth and the regional and community environment of his early years. At least indirectly, these dimensions of time and space affect his life orientation and work culture by dating and locating the sources and types of influences to which he might be exposed.

The Age Structure of the Catholic College Faculty

The empiric fact is that the Catholic college professor is a relatively young man. The majority of the clerical and lay academicians in the study sample were born during the period 1910-1930. In terms of age, 70% are now between the ages of 30 and 50, 19% are over 50 years of age, and 11%, mainly laymen, are under 30. Undoubtedly this relatively youthful age-structure of the Catholic college faculty is a consequence of the academic market situation which, especially in the post-World War II years, speeded up the invasion of Catholic colleges by newly graduated lay professors. As the age distribution of the Lazarsfeld and Thielens sample indicates—64% between 30 and 50 years of age, 27% over 51, and 8% aged 30 or less—the Catholic faculty here studied is only slightly younger than their colleagues in

other American universities.[3] More immediately important, however, are the implications of this age profile in terms of understanding the Catholic faculty situation and of projecting its
future composition and professional status.

First, it is clear that a significant proportion of the Catholic
academic men are the social and intellectual products of an
historical period in which Catholic higher education for men was
still experiencing the traumas of reorganization. They were
graduates of the classes of 1930 to 1945 who were taught for the
most part by religious without advanced degrees and with little
interest in research and publication. The significance of these
educational experiences on the career perceptions and academic
values of today's Catholic academicians will concern us later.
Here they are indicated mainly to give a dimension of time to
the composite social profile.

A second implication of the age distribution of the Catholic
college faculty looks to the future. This is bound to be an "iffy"
implication, but historical evidence and actuarial tables tend to
support it. Thus, if the Catholic college faculty members as
presently constituted in age persist in their academic careers, and
if they enjoy the life expectancy projected for them, over 80%
will remain on the staffs of Catholic colleges for the next 15 to
30 years.[4] This projection is supported by the personal as well
as institutional pressures to faculty stability[5] and by the relatively
high life expectancy prospects of the academic profession, especially among the religious.[6] Unless a continued rate of institutional growth creates new openings, the profile of the Catholic
college faculty will not change significantly for the next twenty
years. In the perspective of time, it is a faculty recruited to
staff the post-World War II expansion of American Catholic
colleges and universities. The composition of its religious and lay
members reflects both the recruitment pressures and the value

transitions which developed in Catholic colleges during this
period.

The Ecological Origins of the Catholic College Faculty

A different set of influences may be tentatively inferred from
the ecological origins and mobility of the Catholic academician.
The regional stratification of the collegiate sample and the limited
possibilities of mobility for the religious members of the faculty
are factors of importance. They do not, however, affect the fact
that 88% of the faculty are native-born Americans and that the
12% who were foreign-born are composed mainly of European
Catholic academicians who fled their native lands during and
immediately after the war. The native-born Catholic professors
have, especially in the case of the religious, remained to teach
in the regions of their birth.

This pattern of regional stability is broken only by the 26% of
the lay professors born in the East and 33% born in the Midwest
who have relocated out of their native regions. Whether this is
a high or low rate of regional mobility for American academicians
must remain unanswered, because no comparable data are available for the non-Catholic group. But the impression persists
that it is a relatively low rate, and reflects a personality structure
in which the positive evaluation of family and other particularistic ties inhibits the openness of the Catholic academic man to
relocation opportunities. Moreover these opportunities are fewer
than those available to his non-Catholic colleagues because of
the smaller world of Catholic higher education.

At a more specific ecological level, the data also identify the
Catholic academic man as the product of an urban culture.
Thus, 36% were reared in a large metropolis or its suburbs, 10%
came from a farm or village setting, and the remainder in almost

equal proportions originated in towns and cities over and under 25,000 population. This urban pattern is consistent with the general demographic picture of Catholic population distribution in the United States. Its significance as a variable in our analysis is not specific because of the predominantly urban culture of American society as a whole. Indeed the only selectivity apparent is the relative absence of the rural born on the staffs of the larger universities and their concentration in medium-sized and small colleges.

THE SOCIAL SETTING OF THE FAMILY

On a more direct and specific level the Catholic academic man is the product of the immediate environment of his family. This environment is so complex and variable that its impact inevitably has its unique aspects. To the point, however, that the general outlines of the environment may reflect common and similar sources and types of influence, they do provide general points of departure for the analysis of the initial and basic socialization of the Catholic academicians as a group. On bases at once related to socialization theory and to practical research conditions, the family-variables here described include: ancestral origins, parental education, religious affiliation, parental occupation, and social class. There is no easy formula for defining the range of family-variables and weighing their relative importance, but is it safe to propose that the ones here described bear, singly and in combination, significant consequences for the professional academic role.

Parental Origins

From the biographical information provided by the research sample it is clear that the native-born, urban Catholic academician is only two generations removed from immigrant status. Almost 50% of the faculty were the descendants of foreign-born grandparents on both paternal and maternal sides, while another 23% had only one or two native-born grandparents. Only 18% traced their American roots back through two generations on both sides of their families. Comparable data for non-Catholic academicians are not available, but demographic materials suggest that the cultural backgrounds of Europe are closer to the Catholic professors than to their non-Catholic fellow scholars.

Relative to the socialization process the more important data are those describing the distribution of the ethnic backgrounds of the grandparents. Unfortunately, the questionnaire elicited this information only for the foreign-born parents of the faculty.[7] This proved to be less than helpful because almost 75% of the faculty sample were brought up in families in which one or both parents were not foreign- but American-born. This fact describes the Catholic academic man as the product of a first-generation American family but does not identify the particular cultural backgrounds of his parents. On the gross evidence of family name, however, and on the statistical distribution of foreign-born parents by nation, it appears that the Catholic academic group was directly and indirectly socialized within cultural frameworks which were, in rank order, Irish, Italian, Polish and German.

The prominence of the Irish origins of so many of the Catholic professors is especially significant because some limited research bases are available for describing the Irish family system and its socializing effects on the child. Typically it has been described as an authoritarian-type family in which the mother plays a powerful role and in which dependency is fostered and security is set as a major goal. Such an oversimplified characterization clearly distorts, even as it illuminates; but it does suggest the kinds of orientation and role perception at least indirectly present in many cases to the formation of the basic personality structure.

Parental Education

A more specific index of the family environment of the Catholic academic group, as it relates to their professional careers, is the educational attainments of their parents. These were understandably conditioned by the educational values and opportunities of their childhood and by their near-immigrant and class status. As Table 2 indicates, these were generally unfavorable conditions, since 44% of the fathers and mothers of the Catholic academicians had no formal education beyond elementary school.

Table 2.—Levels of Educational Achievement of Parents of Catholic Academicians by Religious - Lay Status

Highest level of schooling attained by mothers and fathers		Numbers			Percentages		
		Rel.	Lay	Total	Rel.	Lay	Total
8th grade or less	mother	52	63	115	51.5	39.4	44.05
	father	49	66	115	48.5	41.25	44.05
Some high school	mother	17	31	48	16.8	19.4	18.38
	father	15	29	44	14.8	18.13	16.85
High school grad.	mother	15	37	52	14.8	23.1	19.93
	father	11	22	33	10.9	13.75	12.64
Some college	mother	7	16	23	6.9	10.0	8.82
	father	5	19	24	4.9	11.87	9.19
College grad.	mother	3	8	11	3.0	5.0	4.22
	father	4	7	11	4.0	4.37	4.24
Master's or	mother	—	1	1	0.0	.6	.38
professional degree	father	8	8	16	7.9	5.0	6.14
Doctorate	mother	—	—	—	0.0	0.0	0.00
	father	3	3	6	3.0	1.87	2.29
Don't know	mother	5	2	7	5.0	1.2	2.68
	father	4	4	8	4.0	2.5	3.06
No answer	mother	2	2	4	2.0	1.3	1.54
	father	2	2	4	2.0	1.26	1.54
TOTALS	mother	101	160	261	100.0	100.00	100.00
	father	101	160	261	100.0	100.00	100.00

Another 38% either attended or completed high school but went no further, to make a non-college category of over 80%. Perhaps the most striking statistics, in the light of the general working-class image of the Catholic population, are those describing 21% of the fathers and 13% of the mothers as one-time students or graduates of colleges and universities. This proportion is probably skewed somewhat by the members of the sample who were refugee scholars, converts from non-Catholic families, and the younger members of the family. For the native-born, "cradle" Catholic members of the staff, the proportion is probably closer to Fichter's 1950 data which identify 12% of the fathers of seminarians as attaining college-level education.[8] The somewhat special case of the Catholic professor's family environment in this respect appears when the educational attainments of their parents are compared with those of the parents of non-Catholic professors. Again, the data are limited but revealing. Thus, Eckert and Stecklein report that 27% of the fathers and 19% of the mothers of Minnesota college professors had attended college; and Gustad's data identify 30.1% of the fathers and 31.5% of the mothers of his Southern college professors as college-educated.[9]

The net finding here is that, in a greater proportion than their opposite numbers in non-Catholic colleges, the Catholic professors are generally the first members of their families to attain the level of a college education. They are a first generation of college-educated Catholic Americans and they bring to their professional roles an educational tradition which has begun with their own careers.

Religious Affiliation

Perhaps the least surprising finding concerning the family setting of the Catholic professors is the religious affiliation of their parents. Thus 88% of the mothers and 85% of the fathers were born and brought up as members of the Catholic Church. The minority of professors who had one or both parents non-Catholic is a somewhat larger proportion than one would expect in a group now so closely associated with the teaching mission of the Church. In these cases, exogamous marriages were apparently involved, since 41% of the non-Catholic fathers and 38% of the non-Catholic mothers were later converted to Catholicism. The net result is that all but 5% of the faculty sample were "cradle Catholics," that is, baptized as Catholics and brought up in the atmosphere of a religiously integrated home. The socialization implications of the family's religious life will concern us later in this chapter. The significant statistical finding here is that, unlike the more differentiated religious background of the non-Catholic college faculty, those who teach in the Catholic college are the products of a common and life-long set of religious orientations rooted in their families.

Socio-Economic Status

At a still different level, the Catholic academicians are what they are because of sub-cultural influences related to the socio-economic status of their families. The measures of this status and its socializing consequences are necessarily incomplete and vary in their significance by region and historical period. At a gross but useful level, however, an adequate basis for interpretation of such influences is provided by discrete data concerning the occupation of the father, income, housing, and self-evaluation of class position.

Table 3 summarizes the data describing the occupations of the fathers of the Catholic faculty members. The majority, it is clear, were not professional persons but, against the backgrounds of

their ethnic origins and educational attainments, they emerge as
a group who must have been relatively successful in their pursuit of socio-economic mobility. Thus 22% of the fathers were

Table 3.—Occupations of Fathers of Catholic Academicians
by Religious - Lay Status

Occupations of Fathers	Numbers			Percentages		
	Rel.	Lay	Total	Rel.	Lay	Total
Professional, technical, kindred workers	11	17	28	10.9	10.6	10.7
Managers and officials	30	28	58	29.7	17.5	22.2
Clerical	3	12	15	3.0	7.5	5.7
Sales	7	21	28	6.9	13.1	10.7
Craftsmen, foremen	15	28	43	14.9	17.5	16.5
Operatives	6	6	12	5.9	3.8	4.6
Service workers	10	14	24	9.9	8.8	9.2
Laborers	12	17	29	11.9	10.6	11.1
Farmers	7	13	20	6.9	8.1	7.7
Not classified	—	1	1	—	.6	.4
No answers	—	3	3	—	1.9	1.2
TOTALS	101	160	261	100.0	100.0	100.0

managers or officials, another 33% were "white collar" employees,
and only 35% had jobs as operatives, service workers, laborers,
and farmers.

Compared to the occupational distribution of American Catholics calculated by Stouffer, the fathers of the Catholic academicians appear to have been a more socially mobile group.[10] This
is particularly indicated by the proportion who were in managerial and supervisory positions. It is reasonable to infer from this
that many Catholic academicians were influenced in their educational and career decisions by a mobility environment. There is

a priori evidence to the effect that the mobility goals presented were more likely to be related to law and medicine than to education, but this is not the present concern. It is enough to learn here that Catholic academicians were socialized in a family setting in which occupational mobility was projected as a goal worthy of effort.

This picture of a mobility-oriented family setting is reinforced by data related to other socio-economic indices. Thus, while they were still under nine years of age, 50% of the faculty sample lived in homes owned by their parents. This proportion reached 66% when they were between nine and sixteen years old. Moreover, in terms of family income, relatively few were in extremely depressed circumstances. Many of the faculty respondents were uncertain of their parents' early financial situation, but 18% "felt" that their fathers earned over $6,000 a year while 64% identified their father's income as between $2,000 to $6,000 per year, and only 13% earned less than $2,000.

These details of father's occupation, housing, and income probably explain, too, the self-rating of family class made by the faculty respondents. Thus, 55% of the sample identified themselves as of middle-class origin, 35% preferred the identification of working class, and only 6% and 2% respectively conceived of their families as in the upper and lower classes. These evaluations are vulnerable to distortions which derive from selective recall, romanticization, etc. Generally, however, the consistency of the separate indices with one another suggests that Catholic professors are the sons of socially mobile parents and were socialized in a family setting which was relatively distinctive among American Catholics.

The selectivity of the family origins of the Catholic academicians is largely an intra-Catholic population fact. This is indicated by research data describing the occupations of the fathers of a national sample of American social science professors of whom only 12% were Catholic.[11] The degrees to which comparability is affected by the sample's inclusion of female faculty and its restriction to social science professors can not be predicted. It is unlikely, however, that these factors would explain the sharp differences between the occupational backgrounds of the fathers of this sample and that of the Catholic professors. These differences highlight the generally higher socio-economic background of the non-Catholic academic population. Over half (56%) came from professional and managerial backgrounds and another 15% came from white-collar and small-business families.[12] As Table 3 indicated, only 32.9% and 16.4% respectively of the Catholic academic group came from these kinds of higher occupational backgrounds.

The differences in the ethnic composition and educational attainments of the parents of the Catholic and non-Catholic samples are, of course, important factors in explaining their occupational distributions. It should be noted, too, that in this context the celibacy of the religious members of the faculty reduces the openness of the Catholic group to intergenerational transmission of academic positions. The lay members of the faculty may have sons who will follow in their fathers' footsteps, but it is unlikely that they will soon produce even the 8% in the Lazarsfeld and Thielens sample of cases where fathers were teachers.[13]

PARENTAL VALUES AND INFLUENCES

The socialization forces present to Catholic academicians in their families are only suggested by the foregoing statistical profiles. The more important data are those which describe more directly the values and attitudes of parents and siblings to which the faculty members were exposed. These inevitably cover a broad spectrum, but their major elements are revealed in the faculty members' own perceptions of their parents' values and influences. The interviews rather than the questionnaires elicited this information and provided a somewhat deeper dimension for interpreting the relationships between family socialization and professional values and attitudes.

Family Size and Birth Order

It will be helpful first, however, to set the stage by describing the size of the family and the birth order position of the faculty respondents. Few of them grew up in the environment of a very small family: only 10% fell into the "only child" category. The median number of children lies between three and four, but another 10% had seven or more brothers and sisters. The larger families were somewhat more common for the religious member of the faculty than for his lay colleague.[14]

A second and somewhat distinctive research finding is the fact that 61% of the Catholic academicians were the first-born child (48.6%) or first son (11.1%) in their families. This distinction of the religious and lay professors by birth order is an interesting phenomenon because it suggests a pattern of recruitment to the academic profession which has not been identified among non-Catholic professors and which, according to Fichter's seminarian study, no longer applies to the religious group.[15] Given the mobility orientation of their families, and the alternative career opportunities in their youth, it is not surprising that so many of the first-born sons should have selected, or been selected by, the religious and academic lives. Not only were they accessible and traditionally prestigeful, but few other occupations compared with the priesthood and the academic life as rapid social escalators for minority and lower-class groups.

Whatever the motives and values involved, the Catholic academicians are the first generation of American Catholic college graduates in their medium-sized families. Moreover, as the first-born sons they began their careers without benefit of the sibling experiences available to many non-Catholic academicians.

The Structure of Parental and Familial Values

The interview data describe the parents of the Catholic academicians as the creators of a family atmosphere characterized by love, self-sacrifice, and strong religious sentiments. The majority of the respondents used this simple and direct language, and in similar fashion identified the more important personal qualities of their parents as they perceived them. Typically, moral qualities were singled out, and these were generally positive in character. Kindly, self-effacing, self-sacrificing, "good," honest—these and similar adjectives were the spontaneous and consistent appraisals. It is possible that the depth limitations of the survey-interview procedure partially explain this moral orientation, but the more obvious conclusion must be emphasized. The Catholic academic men, religious and lay, actually loved their parents and, even allowing for the mellowed and selective quality of their memories, they perceived their mothers and fathers as virtuous and dedicated parents.

This pattern of positive evaluation of their parents did not, however, lead the Catholic academicians to deny the authoritarian structure of their families. Some were constrained to prefix their description of it as authoritarian with such adjectives as "benevolent," "truly Christian," etc., but the dominant picture was one of strict parental authority exercised over obedient children. Empirically this is confirmed by the respondents' evaluations of the degree of supervision exercised over their early lives by their parents. Thus 43.1% felt that they were strictly supervised, 20.3% were supervised in some ways, 4.6% felt that their supervision was no different from that of other children, 10.9% experienced some freedom, 16.1% had quite a bit of freedom, and 5.0% did not answer or could not describe their situation.

On the more specific point of the major authority-figure in their families, the largest single number (42.5%) described their fathers as the head of the family but indicated that their mothers helped to make important decisions. In 9.6% of the cases, the father alone was identified as the definite and sole head of the family, but this direction of authority was countered by the 18.1% who reported that in their families the mother tended to be, or definitely was, the head of the household. Both parents were equally important as authority-figures of 17.4% of the respondents, while another 11.4% either did not respond to this question or were brought up in atypical family situations.

Two questions arise here. How typical is this authoritarian structure of the Catholic academicians' family? What are the socialization implications involved? Briefly, regarding the first question, these data confirm the general outlines of the authoritarian structure of the American Catholic family as described in the research of Miller and Swanson, Lenski, Rosen, and others.[16] Compared to Protestant and Jewish families, the parental sanctions of Catholic mothers and fathers are more stringent, the supervision more strict, and the children more dependent. These and other aspects of the authoritarian tone of the Catholic family were reported to vary by social class and were less prominent in middle-class Catholic families such as those in which the Catholic professors were raised. This variation, however, does not alter the fact of their authoritarian-dependency family situation or of their relative difference in this respect from the sons of

Protestant and Jewish families. As for the socialization implications, the hypothesis of Lenski will in later chapters be put to the empiric test. It will be enough to note at this point that the role internalization learned in such a family structure has been negatively associated with the independence and responsibility required in effective scholarly work.[17]

Looking now to the affective tone of the family, the data reinforce the prominence of the maternal role in this no less than in the authority structure of the family. During their childhood years, that is up to age twelve, almost half (49.4%) of the Catholic professors "felt closer" to their mothers while only 7.1% "felt closer" to their fathers. Another 31.5% felt equally close to both parents, while 6.7% and 5.3% respectively did not feel close to either parent or did not answer this question. These directions of affection, it is interesting to note, did not change significantly during adolescence. At the expense largely of the affectional ties to their mothers, almost 5% more of the faculty reported that they did not then feel close to either parent; and almost 10% felt closer to their fathers. An interesting but unexplainable aspect of these changes is the increase of affective ties with their fathers among the religious professors and the increase in alienation from their parents among lay members of the faculty.

The prominence of mother-son ties among the Catholic academic group confirms a stereotype long held in Catholic circles. It is not a surprising finding, given the traditional values of most Catholic immigrant families and given the father's preoccupation with socio-economic mobility. Moreover, the first-born status of so many of the respondents may have heightened the emotional tone of the mother-son relationship.

These speculations as to the reasons for this pattern of affective ties are less important than its implications. The evidence is still far from complete, but a number of psychological studies indicate that children who are mother-centered tend to be less competitive, less aggressive, less achievement-oriented, etc.[18] Whether or not such correlations are positively present to these cases among the Catholic faculty samples will be investigated in subsequent chapters.

As a final note on the family environment, the religious tone established by the parents is clearly pertinent to the respondents' socialization. Their description of this situation involves no surprises. Except for about 9% who felt that their parents had failed in this respect, they consistently identified their mothers and fathers as at least "good, practicing Catholics," or more positively as "excellent" or "dedicated" members of the Church. They explained these evaluations mainly on the basis of religious practices such as family prayer, daily Mass, etc., but some referred to the inner religious spirit of their parents as most important.

According to their sons, however, the boundaries of the parents' concern with religion were personal and familial. Very few of them were active in parish affairs, and even those who were involved at all appeared not to have played leading parts. Nor could the prominence of strong religious feelings be referred to the presence of priests and nuns among the brothers and sisters of the parents. Somewhat surprisingly, especially in view of the number of religious respondents, fewer than 20% of the sample came from families in which priest-uncles and nun-aunts provided either role models or an immediate vocation climate. Such relatives in religious life, particularly in the necessary absence of parental models, had been assumed as indirectly more important than the evidence suggests. Particularly for the religious members of the faculty, the relative absence of these seems to increase the importance of parental religious influence and of school-related experiences and contacts as natural factors in vocational decisions.

The Educational Values and Attitudes of the Parents

In the more immediate and more directly pertinent area of parental educational values and attitudes, the research data are especially revealing. Limited in their own education, the majority were convinced of its need, if not of its value, and were anxious that their sons should have its advantages. Almost 65% of the respondents reported that their parents positively encouraged them in their college goals, or reported that it was simply assumed that they would go to college. For the other Catholic professors no such positive parental attitude existed. In their cases, higher education was simply not considered, or it was not seen as a realizable goal for their children. For this latter group particularly, the absence of positive parental attitudes meant that non-family influences were most important in developing their educational and career aspirations.

Just what the content of these parental attitudes toward education might have been is difficult to identify. As their professor-sons perceived their parents' values, however, education was mainly perceived in instrumental terms. Forty-two per cent of the parents had purely pragmatic views regarding education, while only 14% perceived it solely in intellectual or cultural terms. For the remainder of the respondents' parents, the pragmatic and cultural values were variously combined and weighted, or other types of values were identified. This distribution of parental values regarding education is not unexpected. Neither the educational attainments of the parents themselves, nor the cultural values of the larger society, provided any basis for emphasizing education as a value in its own right. It was much more simply and directly perceived. Education was necessary if their children were to escape the limitations of their fathers' occupations and if they were to obtain the positions of social prestige and reward.

From the interviews it is clear that this generally pragmatic orientation of the Catholic academicians' parents toward the values of education was rooted in specific and concrete occupational aspirations for their sons. This is indicated in the occupational preferences which 54% of the parents, especially the mothers, directly or indirectly recommended to the Catholic professors while they were still very young. In rank order these parents wanted them to be priests, or doctors, or lawyers.

The common note of these parental aspirations is their professional rather than entrepreneurial classification. As Fichter's data concerning the vocations of seminarians indicate, the prominence of maternal encouragement to the priesthood is not new or different.[19] For the lower-class immigrant family the priest-son was not only symbolically significant; the priesthood was also a sure and rapid social escalator for the son and for the family in the community. Similarly, medicine and law were attractive professions because they were accessible, prestigeful, financially rewarding, and socially respected.

It is also interesting to observe that each is a service-oriented profession and that such a direction of parental preference not only points to the range of parental experience with higher-ranked occupations but also reflects some of the work values in which their children were socialized. The small proportion of the parents who perceived teaching as a career for their sons is symptomatic, too, of a utilitarian bias and of an experience in which those who taught were identified more as religious than as teachers.

Summary

As a group, the Catholic academicians are the eldest sons of first-generation, native-born, urban Americans. Their parents tended to be mobile, lower-middle- or working-class persons who had seldom enjoyed more than elementary school education. Their fathers were more often than not the formal heads of their families, but in authority as well as in affection their mothers tended to be the stronger personalities. Typically they were brought up in homes marked by a quite strong religious spirit and were supervised closely in their daily lives by either or both parents. Moreover, education was defined as desirable, especially for its job values, and encouragement was provided for their educational aspirations. For many of the faculty, the career preferences of their parents were unknown, but almost 50% of those identifying parental aspirations indicated a marked service orientation in the projections of priest-son, doctor-son, and lawyer-son.

These notes do not exhaust the list of direct and indirect socializing forces to which the Catholic academicians were exposed. Moreover, there is only incomplete evidence to indicate that these influences were different from those in the socialization of non-Catholic professors. A developing body of psychological and sociological research evidence concerning the socialization background of those who are achievement-oriented suggests, however, that the roles and motives internalized by the Catholic academicians in their family environments were not congenial to the ideal requirements of the professional role of the academic man. Whether or not these familial influences did, in fact, prove dysfunctional for the professional performance of the Catholic college faculty members will be the concern of subsequent chapters.

IV

THE STUDENT LIFE OF
THE ACADEMIC MAN

Student suspicions notwithstanding, the faculty members of Catholic colleges were at one time, indeed for a prolonged time, students themselves. If on occasion they seem to have forgotten this period of their lives, their amnesia only proves that they, too, are human. Sociologically, what they are as professors is an extension of the socializing experiences and influences to which they were exposed in their student days.

This general socializing function of the school has been the subject of much sociological research and analysis. In the case of the academic man it is a process in which the preparation for adult occupational roles is not remote, generic and indirect but immediate, specific and direct. Whether or not he then knows it, there on the other side of the desk are the role models of his future occupation. Indeed, there are few, if any, contemporary professions that compare with the academic in the duration and in the character of the role socialization to which its recruits are exposed. Some occupations may be chosen only during or after adolescence and without the opportunity for much direct observation or experience with their role content. The career decision of the academic man, regardless of its motivation, can hardly be an uninformed choice. Indeed his contact with the role of the teacher is not only more frequent than his contact with any other occupational role but, measured in time, it may be greater than his contact with his own parents.

This unique fact underscores the formative significance of the educational background of the Catholic academic man. His professional values, attitudes, and patterns of behavior are rooted in a personality initially and broadly structured by his family socialization, but their specific forms and their intensity derive more immediately from the role models present to his student life. His perception of the academic role, his ordering of its components, his views of the student, his standards and style, all express the selective influence of one or more teachers whom he has known in elementary and high school as well as in college and university.

The structure of these socializing experiences for non-Catholic academicians requires few, if any, differentiations according to the level of education. The same is true for Catholic college professors, whether religious or lay, in their pre-college schooling, but special features of seminary education require some distinctions at the collegiate level. In the following sections, therefore, the profile of the Catholic academic man will acquire further dimensions by describing the major features of the pre-professional role socialization present in the following stages of his student days: (a) pre-college schooling; (b) college and/or seminary education; (c) graduate study.

THE PRE-COLLEGE STUDENT DAYS

Elementary School

The first important fact is that 67% of the faculty respondents are the products, for the most part, of Catholic elementary schools. As Table 4 indicates, 52% of the sample attended only Catholic grade school, but this proportion is increased by the 15% who, as the interview data reveal, began in public schools

Table 4.—Type of Pre-college Education of Catholic
Academicians by Religious - Lay Status
(Percentages)

Type of School	Elementary			Secondary		
	Rel.	Lay	Total	Rel.	Lay	Total
Catholic and public	18.8	13.1	15.3	6.9	3.8	5.0
Catholic only	67.3	42.5	52.1	81.2	45.0	59.0
Public only	12.9	42.5	31.0	7.9	45.6	31.0
Private	—	1.3	.8	—	3.1	1.9
Other	1.0	.6	.8	4.0	2.5	3.1
TOTALS	100.0	100.0	100.0	100.0	100.0	100.0

for various reasons but received most of their elementary education in parish schools. If we compare this to the Rossis' projection of 50% as the proportion of American Catholics so educated, we find that we have ascertained a stronger identification of the Catholic academic sample to the Church-sponsored schools; we also find that the sample's class position is generally higher.[1]

This is especially evident in the data distributing the proportions of Catholic elementary schooling according to whether the professors are religious or lay. Thus, 86.1% of the clerical members of the sample as compared to 55.6% of the laymen were primarily Church-educated while more than two-fifths of the latter and only 12.9% of the former attended public elementary schools only. This distribution confirms the data of other studies which positively correlate parochial school education with the incidence of religious vocations.[2]

More importantly, it indicates that the religious and lay members of the faculty were exposed in these early years to different educational climates and to role models different in several important respects. This observation does not ignore the many and basic similarities in public and parochial school education, but it does recognize what the Rossis' survey describes as the different consequences of parochial and public school education on the values and attitudes of Catholics.[3] The Rossis' data do not bear directly on academic values and attitudes, but the research fragments of other studies and the generally recognized differences in value structures and teacher models that exist between parochial and public schools dispose us to expect somewhat different socialization consequences. These considerations, it should be recognized, have no reference to the quality of the education and teaching, but to the more general school environments and to their variable implications for the formation of professional values, attitudes, and patterns of behavior. On this level it may be fruitfully hypothesized that the professional products of parochial and public schools will be different.

Whether in parochial or public school, however, the Catholic academicians were, for the most part, models of the scholastic excellence they now seek in others. According to their own recollections, 67% were usually in the top tenth of their classes while only 12% ranked themselves below the top third. The specific meaning of these early records of academic success cannot be precisely evaluated without information as to the standards of the school, the size of the classes, etc. These considerations aside, it is clear that the majority were excellent students and that their academic successes were not indifferent factors in their professional aspirations and formation. At the very least, their aptitudes were bound to attract the interest and encouragement of their teachers and to qualify them for considering academic as well as other professional careers.

In the light of these careers the significance of their parochial school environment and their academic achievements is witnessed in the generally non-academic but religious honor enjoyed by so many as altar boys. In the Catholic parish these boys are generally chosen from the parochial school registrants on bases more religious than academic. Their simple but religiously important function is to represent the congregation by orally responding to the prayers of the priest at Mass and assisting him in the rituals.

Obviously, the recruitment potential for the priesthood among boys in this role is positive and high. Not all aspire to become priests, but research studies confirm the overall recruitment value by describing the great proportion of priests who were altar boys.[4] Among the Catholic academic group the same situation obtains. Thus, 77% of the religious and 56% of the lay members of the faculty reported that they had served as altar boys during their elementary school years and beyond. The significance of their altar boy experiences and satisfactions relative to other factors cannot be guessed. The evidence that 28% of the Catholic professors, religious and lay, identified the priesthood as their early career goal is positive evidence of the altar-boy-priest recruitment pattern and of the early age of this career decision. Whether they perceived the priest as also an academic man is doubtful, since the parish clergy were their more prominent models and these priests were not associated with formally academic functions. This fact aside, the persistence of these eighth-grade religious vocations is established by the evidence that 73% of this number are priests and brothers today. It is noteworthy, too, that no other career then attracted even 10% of the respondents, although teaching was, especially among the lay members of the sample, beginning to emerge as a possible career direction.

The statistical description of the Catholic academic men during this period does not adequately portray the more subtle and significant aspects of their personalities, nor the impact of their educational experiences. The interview material is in this respect more valuable. Each respondent, of course, addressed himself somewhat differently to the questions, and in each case somewhat distinctive features and emphases appeared. As a composite impressionist sketch, however, the following reconstruction of the interview materials highlights the major personality characteristics of the Catholic academic man as a schoolboy.

I was a good student in grammar school and I guess I was what you would call a good boy. I always liked going to school, and most of the nuns I had as teachers encouraged me and guided me. They were generally pretty strict, but this didn't bother me because I liked and respected them. As usual some of them were good teachers and some were not, but all in all I think that I got a good education. Also, I was an avid reader of the local library's books, but they were the usual boy's adventure stories more often than they were more serious things.

Outside of school I just played or fooled around with my brothers and with the other boys who went to school with me or lived in my neighborhood. Most of them were Catholics like myself and in much the same circumstances. Sometimes I earned a little money selling papers or caddying or doing odd jobs, but this wasn't required at all by my parents.

All in all I had a good childhood. I was close to my parents, we had a strong religious life, and I was satisfied because I was doing well in school and got the praise of my parents and teachers. I really didn't know then what I wanted to be and nobody pressed me to decide, but I was quite sure that I'd get to college and I was more or less thinking of the priesthood.

The profile, thus described, is much less than complete. Even so, the childhood and early school experiences of the Catholic academicians are seen to be dominated by values, attitudes, and patterns of behavior which are significantly related to distinctive patterns of role internalization. They were secure and successful, religious and righteous, content and conservative. No single word can epitomize their outlook, but "bland" comes close, because it underscores the undisturbed, unaggressive, unchallenged structure of their home and school environments. The question is, what career consequences have followed from this school socialization?

On to High School

For the majority of the Catholic professors interviewed, the transition from elementary to high school did not involve many important changes in their socialization environment. In a word, the situation was much the same only more so. As Table 4 indicates, almost 70% matriculated in Catholic secondary schools, while only 30% completed this phase of their education in the public school system. As with their elementary schools, the lay academicians were drawn in almost equal number to each type of school, but 88% of the clerical professors received all or part of their secondary schooling under religious auspices. Indeed for 25% of the religious and for 6% of the lay professors the religious auspices were explicitly vocation-directed, since they were enrolled in minor seminaries. Some, of course, did not remain in these, but at graduation from school 38% of those with career plans (four-fifths of the sample) aspired to the priesthood, an increase of 10% (from a generally larger proportion of career preferences) over the number so oriented at the completion of grammar school. It is clear, of course, that these "vocations" to the priesthood were not uniformly perceived and were sometimes lightly, sometimes tightly, held. This is less important than the fact that the familial and educational socialization of the Catholic academicians provided the basis for attracting them as boys to such a service-oriented role as that of the priesthood.

As Fichter's data confirm, the Catholic high school was especially suited to the encouragement of this career direction because its teachers were generally male religious and its curriculum was almost exclusively college preparatory.[5] The priests, brothers, and scholastics were masculine role models with whom the sons of the religiously-oriented, socially mobile, pro-education Catholic parents could readily identify. In addition the tuition expenses involved, while seldom high, tended to make the student body selective and to provide relatively small classes in which there was much student-teacher contact.

In spite of the urban location of these Catholic secondary schools, approximately 50% of the sample graduated in high school classes with fewer than 100 seniors and only 9% graduated in classes numbering over 300 students. The relative smallness of the classes, the omnipresence of the religious teachers, the religiously structured symbolic relationship of Father or Brother to son, these and other factors provided an environment in which role relationships tended to be more diffuse and particularistic than specific and universalistic. The positive functions of this Catholic secondary school setting for the socialization of Catholic professors should not be ignored. But they may have exacted costs in terms of the internalization of the functionally specific, universalistic, affectively neutral, and performance-oriented role expectations of the academic career.

Again the more substantial evidence on this point is provided in the interview material. The more common notes are those described by the following composite spokesman for the faculty.

I enjoyed high school. Most of the time I made the honor roll and this, of course, helped, but they were happy and busy days in other respects, too. I've always felt that I got an excellent high school education from the religious, but I recall most vividly the tight discipline of the place. Some of the teachers were pretty deadly and we probably got too much of the humanities and too little mathematics and science; but in the balance it was a good preparation for college. Looking back at it now, of course, I didn't make the most of it and I wasn't forced to. Maybe it was because I did pretty well in most subjects but I was only "going to school." I was never really worked hard enough, and there was little opportunity for independent work.

Of course, there were the extra-curricular activities, too. I was active in debating and dramatics and put some time in on the school paper, language clubs, sodality, etc. I used to work week-ends and summers if I could do so. It was a busy enough period. Most of my friends were classmates, but we didn't date until we were Juniors or Seniors. I don't think I went to more than one dance until my Senior prom. I was still thinking of becoming a priest and this made a difference but. . . .

No, I didn't have any real problems in those years. Keeping out of trouble was not difficult for me and I enjoyed the activity, the security I had, and my successes in school.

This reconstruction of the major patterns of the Catholic professors' high school days once again oversimplifies and distorts to some degree. The dominant notes, however, are faithfully represented. They describe the Catholic academicians at this age as a group still imbedded in environments which were protective rather than competitive and dependence- rather than independence-oriented. It is quite likely that many of their non-Catholic colleagues were similarly socialized, but in the absence of comparable empiric data this can not be confirmed. On presumptive evidence alone it would seem likely that, in degree at least, the Catholic professors were less exposed to professional values and models.

COLLEGE AND SEMINARY DAYS

The post-secondary-school education of Catholic academic men presents a picture unique among American college and university faculties. The most distinctive feature is the fact that a sizeable proportion of the Catholic college professors did not, in the conventional sense, "go to college." Almost all of them, it is true, have undergraduate degrees, but some are degrees earned in the specialized educational setting of religious houses of study or seminaries. Many continued their studies in other institutions, but for almost 70% of the clerical professors some or all of their college years were spent in the seminary. Consequently, unlike their lay and non-Catholic colleagues, this important group had little or no personal experience with the academic and non-academic life of the students whom they now instruct.

The implications of seminary education on their later roles as professors are relevant but complex considerations. For the most part it was vocational education, in the broadest sense, because its goal was the preparation of the seminarians for the spiritual as well as the professional requirements of religious life. The curriculum was prescribed and was weighted in the direction of sacerdotally relevant subjects such as dogmatic theology, moral philosophy, canon law, etc. The faculty members were almost always priests and brothers who were, at the same time, religious colleagues sympathetic to the seminarian's vocation goals. And the student life of the seminarian was remarkably unlike that of his collegiate peers. In the interests of conditioning him for his future religious roles, he was physically isolated from any commerce with the secular world and he was positively trained in values, attitudes, and patterns of behavior defined as essential to his personal sanctification and professional performance. In the first instance he was being trained to be a priest or a brother and not to be an academician.

This characterization of the educational goals and setting of the Catholic seminary should not be viewed as precluding the possibility of finding there an intellectually sophisticated milieu. In the sacred sciences, especially, the professors were the intellectual elite of the congregation. Frequently they were spotted and marked for posts on the seminary faculty while they were themselves seminarians. Typically, too, they were sent for their advanced studies to the leading American or European Catholic universities. In the sacred areas of their competence these men were at once priests and scholars; but they seldom taught their specialties to the Catholic college student, and in the seminaries their influence was limited institutionally by the pressures of other requirements of seminary life and by the intellectual potential of their seminarian students. Some were effective academic role models for the seminarians and contributed to the development in them of genuinely professional values and attitudes. Their successes in this respect were often achieved in spite of, rather than because of, the usual seminary culture. This culture varied, too, by seminary administration from intellectually hot to cold, but the predominant values did not support the idea of knowledge as an independent value. The seminarian was taught what he would need to know as a priest.

This general picture of the seminary as the pre-professional educational setting for the clerical professors in Catholic colleges is moderated in congregations which have traditionally been identified with educational activities. The Jesuits, for example, are well known as educators, and the environment of their seminaries often reflects the prospective teaching careers which lie ahead of the seminarians. In addition, the choice of a congregation is seldom made without foreknowledge of possible priestly assignments. This is indicated statistically in the evidence that, at the time they entered religious life, 48% of the religious academicians "definitely hoped for a teaching assignment," another 32% were agreeable to this or indifferent, and only 18% did not

want to teach or hoped for some other type of religious assignment. The majority, therefore, are not reluctant professors, but
chose their congregations with the clear knowledge of, and generally with the preference for, their combined role of priest-
professor.

Except for the lay members of the faculty who had tested their
vocations and had left the seminary, the other members of the
sample (religious and lay) spent their undergraduate years in the
conventional collegiate setting. Again the pattern of preference
for Catholic schooling is conspicuous. More than 77% of the total
sample received their degrees from Church-related institutions,
while only 19% are undergraduate alumni of non-Catholic institutions. The remainder held no undergraduate degrees or did not
answer this question. In the light of their elementary and secondary school backgrounds this distribution is not surprising
though the question, why? remains interesting.

The problem of choosing a college did not, as a rule, confront
the religious members of the faculty. They simply went where
their religious superiors sent them. The lay professors, on the
other hand, made these choices on the basis of factors relevant
to their individual cases. The research data indicate that, in the
majority of cases, the choice was not the result of positively defined considerations but was the inevitable product of one or
two significant factors. Typically, it was "very important" to
them and to their parents that the college be Catholic, that the
tuition be low, and that scholarships be available. Important but
less so than these religious and economic considerations were the
reputation of the college, its location close to home, and the
opportunities for part-time work.

The net impression is quite clear. Most Catholic lay professors
chose their undergraduate colleges under the pressures of a
strong religious orientation and a limited purse. It appears that

the academic reputation of the college chosen was either a luxury consideration or was uncritically accepted as adequate. As the first members of their families to attend college, they had little experience on which to draw and were conditioned by parental concerns and by strong religious socialization in secondary schools to choose a nearby, inexpensive, academically adequate, Catholic college.

These bases of choice appear to have had only limited implications for the Catholic academicians' *post factum* evaluation of their college education. Almost 50% of the 175 faculty members (31 religious and 144 laymen) who evaluated their choices felt that "they made the best decision." Only 17% regretted their choice of college, the remainder feeling either that the decision was a good one or was no better or worse than any other they might have made.

Again, in profile form, the self-image and the reflections of the Catholic professors during this period can be outlined in the following reconstructed interview:

College was more difficult for me than high school, but I still managed to get on the Dean's list most of the time and I graduated with honors. I think that I could have done better, but I wasn't really pushed and I probably spent too much time on part-time jobs and on extracurricular activities. Besides, I still didn't know what I wanted to be. For a while it was the priesthood again, or law, or teaching. I was still "going to school," I guess, but the uncertainty about the future used to upset me sometimes.

The course of studies, you know, was heavy on philosophy, and this cut down the elective courses you could take. And the professors were mostly religious then. Some of them were excellent. They made us work and they really knew their fields. I don't think more than a couple of them wrote and published anything, but they hardly had time to breathe. They used to teach 15 to 18 hours a week, they were dorm prefects, moderators, preachers, etc. I was lucky because a couple of my professors were interested in me and I'm sure that some-how they influenced me to consider teaching as a career. Or maybe I just drifted into the field.

The major notes of this interview data do not indicate many changes in the personality structure or the socialization milieu of the Catholic academicians as college students. They were un-competitive, uncommitted, and uninspired. Their academic suc-cesses were not hard-won but, in the absence of any clear occupational goals, they promoted the prospects of graduate school and the possibility of a teaching career.

GRADUATE SCHOOL

The decisions of the Catholic professors to continue their edu-cation beyond college were seldom clear-cut, personal career decisions. In the cases of the priests and brothers, their individual preferences were considered, but the final decision was made by their religious superiors. The needs of the congregation, the talents and inclinations of the individual priest and brother, the variable policies of successive superiors, the limitations on their residence outside of a religious community; these considerations were prominent in deciding who studied what, when, and where. The interview data indicate that some religious were sent to do graduate study in fields and at universities not of their personal choice. These cases were in the minority, but they clearly show that the decision processes of the religious and lay members of the Catholic college faculty are not in many respects comparable.

The decisions of the laymen were personal and free decisions arrived at just before their college graduation or else after it. Indeed prior to their Senior years in college, graduate study had been seriously considered by only 6 of the 28 religious and by 48 of the 165 laymen for whom such a personal decision was possible. This pattern of relatively late career decisions is not only common to the academic profession but markedly distinguishes it from other professions such as medicine, law, and the clergy.[6] The interesting fact is that, even within the academic profession, the Catholic professors tended to decide on their careers later than the samples reported for Southern colleges and for Minnesota colleges.[7] Some attended graduate school because "they had nothing else specific in mind then" or because their scholastic records earned them scholarships and fellowships and this decided their careers. Most, it is true, enrolled with plans for a teaching career, but the pattern of "drift-choice" is suggested by their vagueness concerning the professional level to which they aspired—that is, high school or college.

This indeterminacy among the Catholic lay professors is partially established by the fact that, at the time they entered graduate school, 60% had the Master's degree as their goal while 40% were planning to go all the way for the Ph.D. This may mean simply that they were focussing on one degree at a time, but it may also prevision the still dimly felt character of their career decisions. Actually, the aspirational level fits quite well the level of degree achievement.

The graduate degree achievements of the Catholic college faculty members and their comparison to other available samples is described in Table 5. The differences in institutional sampling and in the types of faculty members included in these comparative studies make any reliable inferences impossible. In the category of those holding the terminal Ph.D., the Catholic college faculty members with 42% were the lowest group, but the differences here with the Minnesota colleges sample were slight. In fact they disappear when allowance is made for priest-professors in the Catholic college sample who have doctorates in the sacred sciences (S.T.D., J.U.D., etc). The Southern college

Table 5.—Graduate Degree Attainments of Catholic
Academicians and Other Academic Samples

Degrees Attained	S R E B Survey*	Minnesota Colleges Survey**	Catholic Academicians
Ph.D.	81.4	44.4	42.0
M.A. or B.A.	17.2	55.0	48.0
No reply or no degree	1.4	.6	10.0
TOTALS	100.0	100.0	100.0

* John W. Gustad, *The Career Decisions of College Teachers*, Atlanta: Southern Regional Education Board, 1960.
** Eckert and Stecklein, *op. cit.*

sample's clear leadership in the proportion of Ph.D.'s is partly a function of that survey's concern only with such established departments as Chemistry, English, and Psychology.

A more detailed examination of the degree status of the Catholic college professors reveals some interesting facts. First, the increasing professionalization of the faculty is witnessed in the fact that 40% of those without doctoral degrees are at various stages of the completion of this degree's requirements. Secondly, the institutional sources of the graduate degrees earned describe a continuing disposition to study at Catholic universities for the Master's degree but an almost even division of Ph.D.'s and Ph.D. candidates by Catholic and non-Catholic universities. Thirdly, in terms of the religious-lay composition of the faculty, 38% of the religious had Ph.D.'s or S.T.D.'s compared to 48% of the lay professors who were doctors of philosophy. Finally, the majority of the Catholic academic group holding the terminal Ph.D. degree were on the staffs of the large and medium-sized institutions in the Midwest and East.

The reasons for, and the implications of, this distribution of faculty degrees and their institutional sources are many and complex. It is clear that the Catholic academic men included in this study represent the dynamic transition to educational maturity of Catholic higher education. The older professors, especially among the religious, either did not have the opportunity for graduate study or were limited to the Master's degree. For the majority of the laymen, however, the Ph.D. has become a prerequisite for staff appointment or has been defined as an increasingly important criterion for promotion in rank. Under these professional pressures, one generation of lay and religious recruits to Catholic higher education changed the academic stature of the faculty. Even a cursory examination of college catalogues proves that, as late as 1935, only a handful of Catholic professors had earned doctoral degrees. The situation then was only slightly better in many non-Catholic institutions; but the lay invasion of Catholic colleges and the rapid upgrading of the professional training received by religious and lay professors has been a more dramatic development than the change in non-Catholic institutions.

Concerning the quality of their graduate programs of study and the reasons for their choices of graduate schools, the interview materials provided by the Catholic academicians are revealing. Each professor had his choice of graduate school, his degree progress, and his critical evaluation conditioned by unique factors. In more than half the cases, however, the choice of the graduate institution was "very importantly" or "quite importantly" determined by such universalistic criteria as the reputation of the university, the reputation of the department, and the type of courses offered. This was not a luxury enjoyed by the remaining faculty respondents. In their cases these considerations were identified as only "fairly important" or "not important" because the critical factors were the availability of scholarships, or regional, community, religious, or family values. The lay professors were particularly vulnerable to these influences because their decisions had to weigh financial outlays, family obligations, and part-time or full-time job opportunities. Often, of course, it was possible to satisfy these demands and still make a choice based on academic criteria.

The research data also indicate that whatever the basis of their choice of graduate schools, few Catholic academicians had the luxury and freedom of uninterrupted study in pursuit of their highest degree. This was especially true among the post-Master's degree candidates, both religious and lay. More often than not, they taught either full-time or part-time at the college level and thus prolonged for many years the completion of their course requirements. Beyond this, the dissertation was reported as requiring about four years for the majority of the faculty, but approximately 25% were delayed on this final phase from 6 to 15 years. Stated simply, the Ph.D. degree holder among Catholic academicians was usually in his mid-thirties when he was awarded his diploma and had been a faculty member for about five or more years.

In the cases of the religious, this older age was the result of beginning graduate study at an age when many others have finished. Depending on the number of years required by his congregation in seminary studies, the priest degree candidate commenced graduate study at an age no less than 24 or 25 or, in the case of the Jesuits, probably over 30. The lay members of the faculty, on the other hand, were often financially handicapped in persisting in their degree work by the responsibilities of marriage and a family.

Whatever the consequences of their prolonged and complicated graduate student careers on their professional goals and role behavior, the majority of the Catholic academicians had good words

to say about their graduate programs. The Master's degree programs were more generally approved than the doctorate ones,
but the reasons were at once so personal and so academic as to
defy analysis. In almost every case, however, the respondents
identified one or two graduate professors who influenced their
professional growth most importantly. The qualities of these
models were explicitly described as influencing the Catholic
professor's own work and goals. Few, however, for reasons to be
explored later, were disposed, or able, to emulate their professional models.

Summary

The educational socialization of the Catholic academic man
was marked at every stage by a strong emphasis on religious
values and attitudes. He is a product of Catholic schools from
his earliest years through the college and even through graduate
school. He was academically successful at all these levels, but
this success was not the result of strenuous achievements. He
was "going to school" in an environment which did not stimulate
competitiveness and provided little scope and motivation for
independent effort. Throughout he was, in the best sense of the
phrase, a good boy—responsible, obedient, co-operative, and
moderately ambitious. He enjoyed the satisfactions of success
and the approval of his parents and teachers, and he thought
long and prayerfully about the priesthood as a life vocation.
For many this was, in fact, the career to which they turned during, or at the end of, their high school years. The majority
persevered and are priests and professors today. Others tested
their vocations but left the seminary convinced that some other
service-oriented profession was their true vocation.

For them and for other laymen, teaching, especially in a religious setting, was a kind of secondary vocation. The role models of their religious and lay teachers had attracted their respect and sparked their interest. Often they were not sure just what they would be, but in the absence of other career goals their academic successes and their service-oriented personalities tended to push them toward graduate study and a teaching career. Almost half of them overcame the obstacles of a limited purse and of modest motivation and acquired their doctoral degrees. As their many colleagues who are still "candidates Ph.D." attest, it was a long and exhausting academic stretch. They were older and wiser at the end of it, but whether their potential had been activated or killed off in the process remained a question which only their professional performance could answer.

V

CLIMBING THE ACADEMIC LADDER

The products of these home and school socialization processes are the Catholic academic men seen now in their professional careers. Hypothetically, these processes previsioned the form and pointed the direction of their careers. But the measures of proof are the careers themselves. The paths these men have followed, and the pattern they have drawn, not only test the imputed consequences of their home and school socialization, but describe the on-the-job factors and situations which have influenced and still influence their professional perceptions and behavior. In sociological perspective the academic careers of Catholic professors are at once dependent variables and touchstones of the occupational environment of Catholic colleges and universities.

The research questions important to the description and analysis of the Catholic academic men's career histories are numerous and complex. When did they begin their academic careers? Where? Why? What institutional changes have they made and why? What is their academic work load? What professional identifications mark their careers? What contributions have they made to the knowledge of their fields? What institutional and personal factors have colored their values and actions? These questions and others do not exhaust the possible research items, but they provide a working basis for describing the career development of the Catholic academician and for analyzing his professional stature. In addition, they provide for some comparisons with the career histories of non-Catholic academic persons.

In outline, therefore, the research materials descriptive of the Catholic academicians' professional career will be presented under the following classifications: (a) career appointments; (b) the work dimensions of the job; (c) achievement symbols: associations and publications; and (d) the "other" factors: Church and family.

CAREER APPOINTMENTS AND CAREER MOBILITY

At the outset it must be noted that the professional careers of the religious and lay members of the Catholic college faculty have built-in bases for important differences in their patterns of appointment and mobility. Like their non-Catholic colleagues, the Catholic lay professors are free professionals. Each can choose where he will teach and, within limits, what he will teach. He is free to seek and to accept appointment in any college, to change his mind for any reason, even to decide not to teach.

The religious members of the faculty, however, enjoy few, if any, of these rights. Each priest at his ordination and each brother at his religious profession freely abdicates his personal rights to make such decisions, and promises obedience to the decisions of his religious superiors. This does not mean that his personal preferences are either unknown or of no consequence. On the contrary, he is usually consulted about his career and, in some instances, he may even be urged to chart his own academic course. There is no doubt, however, about the locus of the decisive authority. What the religious superior does not decide he must at least confirm, and to this ultimate authority the religious member of the Catholic college faculty must, in obedience, defer. To a substantial degree, therefore, the pattern of his appointments and mobility is drawn by decisions other than his own.

These religious-lay differences are not only a unique feature of the professional careers of Catholic compared to non-Catholic academicians but they distinctively affect the environment of the Catholic college. Whether they be deans, departmental chairmen, or professors of any rank, the religious members of the faculty may be ordered to pack and to leave for another institution with little or no notice and with or without the consent of the president of the college.

Because they are conditioned to expect such reassignments and because their religious vocations subordinate personal and natural considerations to communal and supernatural values, the structured instability of the institutional tenure of the religious professors is probably less dysfunctional in career terms than at first appears. Moreover, in practice, selective rather than wholesale reassignment of personnel is common and seniority in the religious community tends to increase tenure prospects.

The professional careers of the lay faculty members are not directly affected by the non-free status of their religious colleagues. But the omnipresent prospect of changes in the composition of the religious administration and the religious staff— changes ordered by extra-university and extra-professional authorities—are unsettling factors that indirectly make a difference in the lay professor's academic career. The non-Catholic academician is exposed, of course, to other types of career-related institutional and extra-institutional forces, but the structured non-freedom of the clerical professors and the indirect relevance of religious authority to the lay professor's career are unique features of Catholic higher education.

The First Rung of the Ladder

The majority of the members of the Catholic college faculty began their full-time academic careers before they had completed their own study for advanced degrees. In effect, they were at the same time, and sometimes in the same place, both professors and students. This pattern of initial appointments is clearly indicated by their degree situations at that time. As Table 6 describes them,

Table 6.—Degree Status of Catholic Academicians at First
Faculty Appointment by Religious - Lay Status

Degree Status	Number			Percentages		
	Rel.	Lay	Total	Rel.	Lay	Total
A.B. only	26	21	47	25.5	12.7	17.6
M.A. in process	3	13	16	2.9	7.9	6.0
M.A. only	36	56	92	35.4	33.9	34.4
Courses for Ph.D.	3	14	17	2.9	8.5	6.4
Candidate, Ph.D.	8	27	35	7.8	16.4	13.1
Ph.D.	26	34	60	25.5	20.6	22.5
TOTALS	102	165	267	100.0	100.0	100.0

17.6% began with only a Bachelor's degree, 40.4% began with M.A.'s in hand or in process, and 13.1% began while en route to the Ph.D. Thus, only 22.5% had the luxury, or the wisdom, to defer their first full-time faculty appointment until they had received the doctorate. Except that there is a relatively high proportion with only an undergraduate degree and a relatively low proportion with Ph.D.'s, this pattern of first appointments is not unique to Catholic college professors. The supply of Ph.D.'s has never been able to match the demands of American higher education, whether Catholic or non-Catholic. The result has been the recruitment of graduate students before they had completed all the requirements for their advanced degrees. There are probably no colleges without their quota of unhappy faculty members who for years have had "everything done but the dissertation."

By contemporary standards, the most striking fact about the

pattern of first appointments in Catholic colleges is the high proportion of the faculty who had only an undergraduate degree at that time. As Table 6 indicates, the majority of these instructors were priests and brothers. This is especially important because it at once suggests the reasons for their appointment without prior graduate study, and it qualifies the critical inferences which otherwise might properly be drawn. Typically, they were appointed to college teaching positions only because the immediate need for their services outweighed the logic which recommended prior graduate study. Moreover, it should be noted that these priests and brothers usually had the advantages of age, experience, and special training not commonly found in the college graduate. More often than not they were in their middle- or late-twenties, they had experience as high school teachers in the humanities, or they were assigned to teach theology or philosophy, areas where, the formality of degrees aside, their seminary education had been most comprehensive. It is not suggested that these constitute adequate substitutes for graduate study, but they do add a corrective dimension to the interpretation of the proportion of religious professors who began their teaching careers armed only with the A.B. It should also be noted that some of the priests also held the ecclesiastical degrees of S.T.L. (Licentiate in Sacred Theology) and that a somewhat higher proportion of the religious than laymen were able to complete their doctorates before accepting their first full-time academic appointment.

The degrees-in-process situation of the lay professors at that time is a commentary both on the rapid growth of Catholic colleges in the post-World War II era and on the vocational values which they had internalized during their family and school socialization. Like most American colleges, Catholic-sponsored institutions of higher learning were hard pressed for staff members when the backlog of five years of college-delayed veterans sought to exercise their government benefits. The available priests and brothers were too few in number and too limited in the range of their subject qualifications. In this situation, the colleges turned to their own graduates of the immediate pre-war years or to other Catholic laymen and offered them faculty appointments. The majority were still graduate students at that time and some were themselves married veterans. They may have still been unsure about their career plans, but in the spirit of "a bird in the hand is worth two in the bush," they accepted, often gratefully, their first faculty appointments.

This pattern of lay appointments to the Catholic college faculty is not surprising for other reasons. Especially in the Catholic communities in which these laymen lived, faculty status in a Catholic college was a rapid social escalator and a source of much prestige and security. Against the background of their own socio-economic situations and uncertain career commitments, the rewards of faculty appointment were not inconsiderable. Moreover, on a different level, appointment was rewarding because the lay faculty member could link his profession to the priesthood in spirit, practice, and association. It was the closest thing available to being a priest himself. As a kind of secondary vocation, it formally identified the lay person with the Church, provided priests as his associates, and satisfied his service-oriented values and needs.

With the advantage of hindsight, many of these Catholic lay professors now express the wish that they had, somehow, completed their graduate studies first. Except for those who have only recently been appointed to the staff, their non-Ph.D. situation has not affected their tenure or its equivalent. But the outside pressures of accrediting agencies and the internal emphasis on professionalization have tended to freeze them in the lower academic ranks and to put limits on their financial expectations.

Their frustrations are often deep and pervasive, but the decisions which lie at the root of them are still defended as necessary; the decision to accept the first faculty appointment is generally perceived as "a good decision," and few regrets on this score are voiced. The professional and apostolic satisfactions of being a faculty member in a Catholic college seem to shine through the financial and career limitations of their positions and to cast a warming glow over their personal and academic lives.

—And There They Stayed

The significant and distinctive sequel to the career beginnings of the Catholic academicians is the pattern of institutional stability which their professional life-histories reveal. Typically, they were either so satisfied with their first appointment or so restricted in their alternative opportunities that there they stayed. For the religious members of the sample, this is indicated in the evidence that almost 70% are still teaching in the colleges where their careers began. Their non-free status and the limited range of alternative appointments open to them make this pattern of stability somewhat less than surprising. The more significant data are those describing 58% and 27% of the lay professors respectively as either still in their institution of initial appointment or in their second institutional setting. Moreover, for 80% of the lay respondents their academic careers to date have been lived exclusively in a Catholic college setting. Only 18% have had prior faculty affiliation with at least one non-Catholic institution.

Comparative data for non-Catholic academicians on this career point are, unfortunately, not available.[1] There is reason to believe, however, that the institutional stability of the Catholic academicians is a relatively distinctive career pattern and that it is related in large part to unique features of the Catholic college environment and of the Catholic professor's market value.

The former factors limit institutional mobility both by restrictive market regulations and by capitalizing upon personal and religious values. The latter factors function to keep academicians in Catholic institutions either because they are professionally less marketable or because the persistence of uninformed stereotypes about Catholic academic persons poses extra and special tests of their professional competence.

The interview materials suggest that the Catholic lay professor's institutional stability derives for the most part from features of his own situation as well as that of the Catholic college. Some feel that their careers are limited to Catholic colleges because the non-Catholic collegiate world thinks often and fearfully before hiring, especially in some fields, Catholics who wear the label of a Catholic college. The evidence in support of this view is, however, seldom provided. The more clear-cut fact is that Catholic lay professors remain in Catholic colleges, and even at the same college, because they want to and because outside this market their professional value depreciates.

The bias of these lay professors for Catholic colleges is not hard to understand. With few exceptions, they have had Catholic schools for their second home from the first grade through graduate school. Sisters, brothers, and priests have been their teachers and friends, and they feel a comradeship with them and with their vocations which inspires a strong sense of loyalty. The sometimes strident criticisms of some lay members of the faculty would seem to belie this affective bond, but, especially in the past, these criticisms were more often in the nature of family squabbles than of professional protests.

The recent and rapid growth of AAUP chapters on Catholic college campuses symbolizes the growth of a more professional orientation,[2] but it is doubtful that it has lessened at all significantly the ties of loyalty that help to bind many laymen to their Catholic colleges. They are daily reinforced by the climate of loyalty and obedience set by the religious members of the faculty and by the explicit and implicit structure of rewards which define loyalty as a premium value in the eyes of the religious administration.[3] The loyal lay-members of the faculty are the regular objects of public praise and are more or less guaranteed a kind of tenure regardless of their degree situations. The religious administrators often seem to feel a more than professional responsibility for their loyal lay associates and the unspoken knowledge of this disposition, and of cases in which it has been proved, further influences the Catholic college lay professor. On these personal and institutional bases, they stay where they are because they want to.

A different type of pressure toward institutional stability derives from the professional status and market value of the Catholic lay professor. Some of those interviewed have professional credentials which would merit appointment in almost any American university. The majority, however, even if they wished to change their academic positions, have little prospect of doing so or of improving their situations. They do not have terminal degrees from prestige universities, or they have no record of successful professional performance, or they are outsiders in the informal leagues of the academic marketplace. Outside the system of Catholic higher education, these factors tend to reduce the professional opportunities and the market value of many lay professors. Their relevance to the pattern of faculty stability, however, is minimal. For the majority, the Catholic college is a second home.

Climbing the Ladder

The institutional stability of the Catholic academicians finds another explanation in the pattern of their rank mobility since initial appointment. Again the picture is complicated by the special situation of the religious, and it is obscured by the absence of comparable data for non-Catholic professors. In spite of this, the major features of the Catholic academicians' career mobility are clearly outlined and are positively related to their institutional stability.

Prior to World War II, academic rank was seldom a formal concern of Catholic colleges or their religious faculty. Typically, the rank of professor was informally assigned to the outstanding clerical scholars and teachers, but it was also a reward for seniority. As symbols, these ranks were appreciated by the religious members of the faculty when and if they realized them. The titles of "Father" and "Brother" were their first claims to identification, however, and in the fraternity of the religious community these did not lend themselves to differentiation.

The appointment of an increasing number of laymen to the faculty complicated this largely unstratified system and required the formalization of a rank structure and of rank criteria. Frequently this task was approached in generous and piecemeal fashion because the market was tight, paternalism was the order of the day, and rank was easier to provide than money. The majority of the older lay-members of the faculty are the beneficiaries of this situation. According to contemporary professional standards, many were not qualified for their promotion to the ranks of associate and full professor. Their promotions were rewards for teaching competence, seniority, and loyalty, and they served to assure a high degree of institutional stability of personnel.

In recent years, the climb up the academic ladder has been more difficult, especially in the larger colleges and universities. There is no system-wide formula, but terminal degrees, publication, and other professional measures or symbols of competence have become of decisive importance. Superior teaching is also included in the promotion equation, but its non-measurable quality has weakened its value as a criterion. This fact and the very speed of the change-over in mobility criteria have been sources of much faculty tension and frustration. For some assistant professors without degrees or publications, the adoption of what they consider to be new ground rules midway in their careers has threatened their security and eliminated their mobility chances. A few years back, their teaching competence, their seniority, and their loyalty would have been rewarded by promotion to the tenure rank of associate professor. Most of them are confident that the administration will provide them with tenure or its informal equivalent as an acknowledgement of the job equity to which their years of service entitle them. But the financial costs of their career immobility are incalculable, their self-images are downgraded, and none aspire to the title of the oldest living assistant professor.

The frustrations of this group are increased when they observe the rapid career mobility of those who, even minimally, satisfy the "new" criteria. Like all other colleges, Catholic institutions are forced to recruit in a seller's market. The young Ph.D. often starts his career as an assistant professor and capitalizes on his market value by "rushing into print" in order to qualify for the associate professor rank. Not all of them succeed, of course, but the career mobility prospects of the lay professors in the Catholic college are promising, if the professors themselves are promising. Their degrees, their minor publications, and their loyalty ease the climb to the senior academic ranks and reward them with the recognition of their in-group peers. They can never aspire to be college president, or even dean, but within the ranks of the instructional staff they can expect both mobility and security.

THE WORK LOAD OF THE FACULTY

The academic work-week provides another angle of vision for the description and evaluation of professional roles. Unlike many other occupations, the details of the work and time expenditures of professors defy any facile classification and summary. Much of their work is cerebral and is unclocked, uncharted, and even unintended. Only a gross profile, therefore, is possible, but even in this form the data are revealing in their content and implications.

Class Loads

During the spring semester of the academic year, 1959-1960, 70% of the Catholic academic men reported that they spent ten or more hours per week in scheduled class meetings. Without the refinements which class enrollment statistics and other data provide, the work meaning of this time expenditure is consider-

Table 7.—Distribution of Weekly Number of Credit Hours of Classroom Instruction of Catholic Academician by Religious - Lay Status

Credit Hours of Classroom Instruction per Week	Numbers			Percentages		
	Rel.	Lay	Total	Rel.	Lay	Total
Less than 6 hours	6	5	11	5.9	3.0	4.2
6-9 hours	37	29	66	36.6	18.0	25.3
10-12 hours	38	88	126	37.6	55.5	48.2
13-15 hours	15	29	44	14.9	18.0	16.9
More than 15 hours	5	9	14	5.0	5.5	5.4
TOTALS	101	160	261	100.0	100.0	100.0

ably obscured. It indicates only that the instructional load of Catholic college faculty members is generally heavy, probably more so than that of their non-Catholic colleagues.

But the distributions of these class loads by the religious-lay status of the faculty member, by academic rank, and by size of college are particularly interesting. On this specific but rough

measure the lay professors have the heavier class loads, since
79% of their number compared to 57% of the religious reported
ten or more class hours per week schedules. It is surprising, too,
to find that these heavier loads are more frequently found in the
medium-sized institutions (76%) and larger colleges and universities (70%) than in the smaller colleges (64%). In addition, senior
academic rank does not, in Catholic colleges, find its reward in
lighter class-schedules. On the contrary, professors and associate
professors in the sample reported an average of 11.5 hours of
instruction per week compared to ten hour programs for
instructors and assistant professors. Finally, the data indicate
that these class loads of the Catholic academicians involve about
three separate courses or preparations. The majority of these are
courses at the undergraduate level, since only 27% of the respondents taught one or more graduate courses.

Non-Class Work Loads

The opinions of many non-academic persons to the contrary,
the instructional load of the college professor does not con-

Table 8.—Distribution of Non-teaching Hours in Work Week
of Catholic Academicians by Religious - Lay Status

Non-Teaching Hours per Week	Numbers			Percentages		
	Rel.	Lay	Total	Rel.	Lay	Total
No hours	15	3	18	14.8	1.9	6.9
1- 5	26	40	66	25.7	25.0	25.3
6-10	19	51	70	18.8	31.9	26.8
11-15	13	27	40	12.8	16.9	15.3
16-20	12	15	27	12.0	9.4	10.4
21-25	9	7	16	8.9	4.3	6.1
26-30	4	8	12	4.0	5.0	4.6
31 and more	3	9	12	3.0	5.6	4.6
TOTALS	101	160	261	100.0	100.0	100.0

stitute his work week. This becomes clear when the data describing the non-class academic work and time expenditures of the Catholic academic men are examined. Again the profile must be recognized as gross because of the complexities of these non-class activities, the inevitable approximations about time expenditures, and the basic differences in the work perspectives of the religious and lay respondents.

Expressed in statistical terms, the Catholic academicians spend an average of about eleven hours per week in such non-teaching activities as student conferences, committees, extra-curricular clubs, laboratory supervision, thesis direction, etc. Individual respondents reported such time expenditures as involving from one to fifty hours per week of their time, but the more common range was between six and fifteen hours. Again, the data identify the lay members of the staff as busier than their religious colleagues in these non-teaching activities. According to their reports, these involved an average of fifteen hours per week compared to a ten-hour weekly average for the religious. The number of these non-teaching commitments and their relative importance in the time expenditure of the professors varied greatly by individual cases. It is significant that the most frequently reported feature of non-teaching time expenditure was that of student conferences. The strength of these student-oriented values of the faculty is indicated in the fact that only 22% of the respondents (36% of the religious and 13% of the laity) did not identify any portion of their work week as expended in this direction. The remainder of the sample (78%) averaged about 4½ hours per week in student conferences.

The cumulative time budget of the Catholic academicians' work load adds little to the foregoing picture. By their own reports the laymen are somewhat busier than their religious colleagues, but the difference is reduced considerably by the time expended by the religious in "other" miscellaneous activities. It should be noted, too, that the non-separation of the religious professor's place of work and place of residence may have compounded for him the problems of approximating at all accurately his extra-class schedule. Unlike the lay person, for whom the professional role is segmental, and therefore more measurable, the total status of the priest tends to merge a wide variety of discrete and different kinds of relationships and activities. There is no direct evidence that these differences in the work perspectives of the religious and lay professors affected their descriptions of their work loads. The impression persists, however, that significant religious-lay differences in total work load are overall not very common.

The absence of details and of comparable data for non-Catholic academic persons makes the foregoing profile of the Catholic professors' work load more descriptively than analytically valuable. Much additional time, it is certain, is expended on research, self-study, lecture preparation, informal seminars, shop-talk, etc. Information on such activities would have been essential in a study with a narrower focus. The present more limited information only suggests that the Catholic academic men are rather heavily committed to class and other student-oriented activities.

Table 9.—Work Load (Class and Laboratory Hours, Moderatorships, Committees, Student Conferences, etc.) for Week of Catholic Academic Man by Religious - Lay Status

Number of Hours	Numbers			Percentages		
	Rel.	Lay	Total	Rel.	Lay	Total
Under 10 hrs.	5	1	6	5.0	.6	2.3
10-19 hrs.	46	68	114	45.5	42.5	43.7
20-29 hrs.	34	57	91	33.6	35.6	34.9
30-39 hrs.	12	24	36	11.9	15.0	13.8
Over 40 hrs.	4	10	14	4.0	6.3	5.3
TOTALS	101	160	261	100.0	100.0	100.0

In the American academic world the more important indices of professional status and career mobility are those symbolized by extra-class and extra-institutional associations and achievements. Success as a teacher and as a worker in the interests of students and the college may be rewarded by local recognition and praise. But achievements in such areas seldom extend beyond these boundaries and acquire professional recognition on the national level. Whether or not this should be the case is a value-loaded question. The facts are that the professional status and career mobility of American academic persons are measured symbolically by membership in professional associations and both symbolically and concretely by professional publications.

Associations and Conventions

The sensitivity of the majority of the Catholic academicians to the symbolic and practical values of professional associations appears in their record of memberships. Just how this record compares with that of their non-Catholic colleagues cannot be evaluated, but 80% of those interviewed were members of at least one national association of academicians. The majority, in fact, were members in two or more such associations but, typically, this included one specifically Catholic association, e.g. The American Catholic Historical Society, etc. Philosophers and theologians were especially prone to limit their professional membership to these in-group associations, but this pattern was prominent, too, among those in the humanities and the social sciences. Historically, the establishment of these exclusively Catholic groupings of professors was motivated not only by the often special research and teaching concerns of their members but by a sense of philosophical defensiveness and professional insecurity. It is an index of the more mature status of Catholic higher education that these in-group associations are less frequently isolated these days from the larger non-sectarian societies and are seldom the center of the Catholic academician's professional identification.

The involvement of Catholic professors in the activities of their professional associations is still relatively modest. What this means against the background of personal and institutional resources and the functions served by annual conventions is debatable. The empiric fact is that 27.4% of the 208 respondent-members of professional societies had not attended an annual convention in the past five years. When the percentage of those who hold no such professional membership is added, the absence of this type of professional contact and interaction is seen to be characteristic of more than 40% of the Catholic college professors.

Partial explanations for this pattern of non-participation are to be found in the non-market status of the religious professors and in the relative inadequacy of personal and institutional resources for such professional activities. It is clear, too, that the non-publication orientation of so many Catholic academicians lessens the prospect of their programmed participation in the convention proceedings and eliminates one source of motivation to attend. By these limited-value measures, the Catholic academic men as a group are still only on the threshold of full identification with their professional roles.

"Publish or Perish" ("or Parish")

The same "threshold" status of Catholic college professors appears in the data describing their records of publication. The reported publications of the Catholic faculty members here studied would seem to belie this observation since the totals included sixty-three books, ninety-eight monographs, and over eight hundred articles. Examined in closer detail, however, these statistics expose both an inflationary factor in the publication data and a disproportionately small number of faculty contributors. The number of articles published, for example, would be considerably less if adjustments were made to distinguish the forty to fifty such publications reported respectively by six foreign-born lay faculty members. Similarly the identification of 35% (36) of the religious and 48% (76) of the lay professors as publishing academicians obscures the fact that for 9 of the former and 22 of the latter, the total individual output was one or two articles and/or monographs. The nucleus of those who publish comprises only one-quarter of the religious and one-third of the lay respondents. This measure, of course, says nothing of the qualitative aspects of their publications. On the gross evidence of the publisher's reputation and/or the type of periodical, it would appear that the majority of the publications of the Catholic academic men are professionally respectable contributions; others, by the same imprecise norms, are less significant.

The empiric proof of the much-discussed non-publication status of Catholic professors is provided by comparative data.

Table 10.—Publication Indices of Catholic Academicians and Lazarsfeld - Thielens Sample (Percentages)

Publication Index	Lazarsfeld-Thielens Sample	Catholic Sample
4,3	46	23
2	25	15
1,0	29	62
TOTALS	100	100

Table 10 identifies the publishing and non-publishing proportions of the sample of Catholic professors studied here and in the Lazarsfeld-Thielens sample of American Social Science professors.[4] Even when allowances are made for the differences in the size and composition of the respective samples, the relative differences in the proportions of Catholic and non-Catholic professors with high publishing indices is striking. Thus, twice as many of the social scientists sampled, or 46% compared to 23% of the Catholic professors, had high publishing indices of 3 or 4. Similarly, indices of 0 or 1 were reported for only 29% of the former compared to 62% of the latter.

The group composition of these publishing and non-publishing Catholic college professors will be investigated later in more detail. Here the data only confirm the speculations and impressions of critical observers of Catholic intellectual life.[5] They further indicate that the sanctions for non-publishing—"perish" for the laymen and "parish" for the religious—have not yet been effectively brought into play. The administrative noises now being made in some Catholic higher education circles portend the increase of non-promotion or dismissal policies for those who do not publish. These "hard" decisions, however, will be difficult to make because the academic market place is tight and because the ties that bind are still more particularistic than universalistic.

THE "OTHER" FACTORS:
CHURCH AND FAMILY

The special case of the Catholic academic man's professional career is highlighted, too, by the other roles which he plays and by the values he attaches to them. The priest-professor, for example, is first and foremost a religious person, an *alter Christus*. His vocation, in a strict theological sense, is to seek personal sanctification and to serve as a divinely chosen agent of God for the salvation of others. The total status-construct of his priesthood integrates his official role as a functionary of the Church and his "other" roles, and posits no conflict between them. This, however, is an ideal construct. In the real order the personality structures of individual priests, the social structure of the Church, and the cultural systems in which these are embedded, all threaten the delicate equilibrium of the total status of the priesthood. More immediately, they are the ideological and environmental referents of the priest-professor's role perceptions and role behavior as an academician. And unlike his lay colleagues, the priest-professor is socially visible and professionally vulnerable to the critical evaluation of many diverse and significant publics. His is the classical case of "the man in the middle."

This structured atypicality of the priest-professor's role does not, of course, formally or directly affect the professional role of his lay colleagues. But it is clear that in varying degrees the same ideological and environmental referents are present and available sources of influence on the lay professor's role perception and behavior. In direct fashion these may be reflected in his perception of the academic role as a kind of "secondary vocation" which unites him to the priesthood and to the mission of the Church and which emphasizes the moral rather than the intellectual components of his role. Less directly, too, these specifically religious values may be perceived as warrants for the subordination of career goals to the prior claims of familial or other responsibilities. In this latter respect the Catholic lay professor's dilemma is not unique. But there is presumptive evidence that the "pull" of these family responsibilities complicates the problems of his dedication to a professional career in a degree greater than that experienced by many of his non-Catholic colleagues.[6]

Priest and Professor

The research questions here focused in one-sided fashion on the implications of the priesthood for the priest-professor's academic career. Posed in an open-ended manner, they evoked responses which ranged from flat denials of the assumption of the question to claims that an academic career is impossible for a priest.

This diversity of reaction is particularly interesting because, with few exceptions, the priest-respondents were members of religious congregations which had long fulfilled teaching functions for the Church. Indeed, 60% of the priests reported that, when they entered religious life, they expected and wanted to play the role of priest-professor. Another 20% noted that they were aware of, but indifferent to, the possibility of a teaching assignment, while 18% entered their congregations expressly hoping for non-teaching priestly functions. At present the vast majority express themselves as dedicated to, or content with, their teaching roles, but a few teach only because they have been so ordered by their superiors. These latter religious would prefer to fulfill their priesthood in parish, missionary, or other activities.

Significantly, the majority of the priests perceived this potential role-conflict in terms which emphasized pragmatic rather than professional considerations. Thus, most did not advert to or even suggest an awareness of role conflict except insofar as their priestly functions posed problems of finding adequate time for their academic roles. They noted in almost every instance that such time-consuming non-academic priestly activities as part-time parish work, counselling, and preaching cut into their work week and lessened their opportunities for scholarly research and publication. This loss was seldom sharply felt or regretted, however, because many enjoyed the satisfactions of the specifically priestly functions of preaching and counselling. Indeed, their academic roles were often perceived as extensions of these preaching and counselling functions of the priesthood. They were priests *and* professors, and they accented the teaching functions of both roles.

The two polar variants to this priest and professor image found little representation among the religious respondents. A few indicated that the fullness of each role was incompatible with the other and that it was almost impossible for the priest to be a priest and an academic professional at the same time. Quite an opposite view was interestingly held by another minority. They identified themselves not as priests *and* professors but as priest-professors. They refused to accept any assumption of role conflict in their cases because, as they viewed it, academic work was their way of fulfilling their priestly vocations. Typically this group of respondents felt that as priest-professors they had a commitment to the research and publication activities necessary for professional growth and development. To this end they sought and often received exemption from some of the more specifically priestly assignments (parish work, retreats, preaching, etc.), or they carefully limited the time and energy directed to these activities. As one respondent put it, "I'm a scientist who happens to be a priest."

The uniqueness of this priest *and* professor or priest-professor role complex in American higher education needs no elaboration. The difference in the modes by which individuals have related their priestly and academic careers reflects not only differences in talent and prior socialization but the basic problem of achieving the role integration of the priesthood's total status. To a substantial degree, too, it provides a structural basis for understanding the disproportionately low amount of published research reported by this group of Catholic academic men.

Family and Profession

For the lay professors in Catholic colleges the extra-academic analogue to the priest and professor complex is the problem of satisfactorily adjusting family responsibilities to the professional requirements for career growth. This problem is, of course, a sociological commonplace and is unique neither to Catholics nor to the academic profession. The key question is whether or not the socio-religious familial values and attitudes of Catholics make a difference in the direction or the degree of their orientations and commitments to their academic careers.

The thinness of the present research materials on this point and the absence of comparable data for non-Catholic professors makes any definitive statement impossible. We know that the statistically typical Catholic lay professor marries in his late twenties or early thirties and is then still in the process of completing his doctoral degree requirements. We know, too, that he now has three or four children, a house complete with mortgage, and a "small" savings account. His wife in 54% of the cases is herself a college graduate (almost half of these also have graduate degrees) but, with few exceptions, she and her non-college wife associates are now full-time housewives. The interview materials also suggest that family responsibilities and family considerations are a significant part of the Catholic lay professor's structure of values. He appeared to be actively involved in time and in spirit with the activities of his wife and children and his career concerns and decisions often reflected the importance he attached to these ties. Thus, he wanted more money to provide a better life for his family, but he was reluctant to follow professional opportunities that would mean separation from relatives and friends. His perception of his role as husband and father seemed to reflect religious and ethnic and class values. He was a professor in a Catholic college and he was a family man.

The undocumented suspicion persists that this sketchy family profile of the Catholic lay professor not only distinguishes him from his non-Catholic colleague but provides an important background for interpreting his professional values and behavior. Random observations and inferences from related studies suggest that the non-Catholic academic man marries at an earlier age, has a smaller family, and is more likely to have a wife who has completed college and graduate study. In the practical order these factors may make less complicating the adjustment of his familial and professional roles and may free him for a deeper commitment to his academic career. Similarly, the relative absence of strong religious, ethnic and social definitions of the husband-father role in the family situations of some non-Catholic academicians provides for an easier emphasis on his rights and duties in the occupational structure. In a relative sense he is freer to accept the demands of his profession and to be more the academician and less the family man.

The tentative character of these observations cannot be overemphasized. At the same time they find support not only in the Catholic ideal of family life taught by the Church but in the empiric research findings of Lenski, Swanson and Miller, and others. These suggest that the socio-religious values central to Catholic family life may, to the degree that they are not neutralized, undercut the career perceptions and career mobility concerns of the Catholic professor by emphasizing the primacy of his responsibilities as husband and father.

Summary

The academic careers of the Catholic academician vary importantly according to their religious or lay status. The majority in both faculty sub-groups began their professional careers before achieving their terminal degrees. The clerical professors seldom had any personal voice in the decisions that led to this condition or to the character of their assignments. Many of the laymen, on the other hand, were recruited to staff the growing post-war college faculties. Few colleges had the luxury of holding out for Ph.D.-qualified professors. They were anxious and pleased to give appointments to young Catholics who were academically talented, available, and inexpensive. Typically, these recruits have remained at the same institution and have provided capable and loyal service. But for many, the premature, even if necessary, acceptance of a faculty appointment has killed off their doctoral degree prospects and has frustrated their intellectual and career potential.

These frustrations are increased by the structure of the Catholic professors' work situations. The majority have relatively heavy class loads and for personality, as well as professional, reasons invest much more time in extra-curricular activities. The combined results of these degree and work situations are that few actively participate in professional associations and the majority have no record of professional publication. Whatever their skill in teaching and in various academic sub-roles, the low estate of their professional achievement in publication terms is an empiric fact and a negative symbol of their stature.

Finally, the careers of these Catholic academic men are seen as uniquely influenced by the significance of their "other" roles. The role-conflict potential built into the dual self-identification of the priest-professor is a personal and professional dilemma for many. Similarly the lay professor's involvement in his family life, while present to non-Catholics as well, often seems to be such a central concern that his professional career is affected. The religious values of the former and the family of the latter make difficult the kind of professional commitment which career achievements require.

PART THREE

THE CATHOLIC PROFESSOR,
IMAGES AND REALITIES

VI

PROFESSIONAL VALUES AND THEIR SOCIAL CORRELATES

Against the background of the foregoing historical and biographical data, it is now possible to analyze the professional stature of the Catholic academic man. How does he perceive his professional role? What professional values are central to his self-concept and to his behavior? What differences in value orientation and behavior can be identified? Why are some professors research- and publication-minded and others teaching- and non-publication oriented? How do the varieties of their socialization experiences relate to their professional values and performance? And how does the institutional setting of their research and teaching affect their role perceptions and satisfactions?

These and other questions probe the images and realities of the professional life of the Catholic academic man. They are questions not easily answered because their terms are so often ambiguous or multivalent and because they have affective overtones that strike notes of different intensity from one man to another. In American academic circles of recent years, the dilemma of the professor pressured to teach *and* to publish has provoked heated debate within and without the university. There is still no consensus, but even this fact is analytically significant.

115

It underscores the need to identify the value orientations of the Catholic professors and to relate these not only to their academic performance but to their prior socialization and work situations. Within the limits of a survey research, this chapter begins this task by describing the research findings in terms of the following categories: (a) professional values, teaching satisfactions, role preferences and value-conflict decisions; (b) the composite value-orientation profile; (c) value orientations and family socialization; (d) value orientations and school socialization; and (e) value orientations and career patterns.

PROFESSIONAL VALUES

The professional values of the academic man inevitably reflect a large and complex number of items of attitude and behavior. What to study, especially in a survey investigation, and how to study it are, therefore, critical research decisions. Here it was decided that a study of the gross problem of teaching and research orientations was both analytically the most important, and technically the most feasible.

In order to evoke, explicitly and implicitly, the value orientations of the respondents, three measures were devised. These concerned respectively: (1) the teaching satisfactions experienced; (2) the academic sub-roles preferred; (3) the decisions made in hypothetical value-conflict situations.[1] The first of these is an independent measure not readily related to the other measures but descriptively interesting in its own right. The other two, however, are so constructed that the separate profiles of the research-oriented and the teaching-oriented professors can be compared and used as the basis for a composite profile. This composite profile balances off the self-image of the professor against the values he manifests in the evaluation of specific problem cases.

Teaching Satisfactions

For Catholic academic men, the teaching process is not only a primary professional activity but a major source of career satisfaction. Table 11 establishes this by summarizing their scaled evaluations of statements describing selected teaching satisfactions. The overall picture identifies the faculty as "agreeing strongly" or "agreeing" with each statement in ratios which range from a low of 68% to a high of 85%. This general pattern of consensus is interesting but perhaps not too surprising.

The more analytically valuable data provide us with the rank order of these teaching satisfactions. The professional image here projected is significantly ambiguous. On the one hand, the teaching functions associated with intellectual values and interests are positively appreciated, in that 85% and 81% respectively classify the clarification and stimulation of their own thought, and the discovery of a few excellent students, as especially rewarding. On the other hand, the high values placed on the moral types of teaching satisfactions are reflected in the fact that 80% find reward in helping their students to achieve moral and emotional maturity, 69% enjoy working with the less apt students, and only 68% are positively disposed to the function of encouraging young people to challenge and to modify their conventional beliefs. These variations, it should be noted, are all within the positive range of "strongly agreeing" and "agreeing" with these statements as teaching satisfactions. The intellectual satisfactions of teaching are dominant, but the prominence of moral satisfactions and moral concerns may express a distinctive orientation of Catholic professors.

Looked at in historical perspective, this ambiguous priority of intellectual over moral types of teaching satisfactions is an index of growing academic maturity. The limits of this maturing process and of the special interests of Catholic higher education

Table 11.—Distribution of Catholic Religious and Lay Academicians' Agreement and Disagreement with Statements of Major Teaching Satisfactions (Percentages)

A Major Teaching Satisfaction is	Strongly Agree			Agree			Combined			Neutral			Disagree			Strongly Disagree			Combined			No Opinion		
	1			2						3			4			5						6		
	R	LM	T	R	LM	T	R	LM	T	R	LM	T	R	LM	T	R	LM	T	R	LM	T	R	LM	T
Working with few excellent S's	42	41	41	35	44	40	76	84	81	6	11	9	8	3	5	4	1	2	13	4	7	5	6	2
Working with less apt S's	26	24	25	45	44	44	71	67	69	11	18	15	10	10	10	2	5	4	12	15	14	6	—	2
Clarifying own thought	43	49	47	42	36	38	84	86	85	9	10	9	1	1	1	3	1	2	4	4	4	3	1	2
Helping S's achieve moral and emotional maturity	58	43	49	23	37	31	81	30	80	7	12	10	3	4	4	—	1	1	3	5	4	9	2	5
Encouraging S's to challenge and modify beliefs	42	34	37	26	34	31	67	68	68	20	20	20	4	7	6	2	2	2	6	9	8	6	2	4

are, however, interestingly reflected in the Catholic professors' evaluations of the satisfaction attributed to encouraging young people to challenge and to modify their conventional beliefs. This teaching function was not only perceived in neutral or negative terms more frequently than any other, but it was considered even less satisfying than working with the slow student.

It was obvious in the interviews that this statement was threatening or disturbing to many of the faculty respondents. Raised eyebrows, perplexed frowns, and oral asides were frequently perceived evidences of discomfort. Some described it as an ambiguously stated satisfaction; others sought to distinguish between the "challenging" and the "modifying" of beliefs; still others expressed their resistance by redefining or qualifying the terms "conventional" and "belief." One could almost see some of the professors mentally substituting the words, "traditional doctrines." Moreover, this morally-oriented disposition was almost equally frequent among the lay and among the religious respondents. It marked, too, not only the attitudes of those neutral or in disagreement with the statement but many who eventually agreed with it as describing a teaching satisfaction.

The value implications of these rankings are necessarily tentative, the more so because no comparable data are available for non-Catholic academicians. At the very least, they identify the problems of value-dualism or value-conflict as persistent and pervasive. From another angle, they describe a system of higher education in process of transition, still groping to redefine its objectives and purposes. It is clearly significant that the majority of the Catholic academic men emphasize the intellectually-oriented teaching satisfactions more than those of a moral type. The fact nonetheless remains that almost one-third of them are more comfortable and more satisfied when their joint adventure with their students in the pursuit of truth is "reiterating" rather than "challenging" and "reinforcing" rather than "modifying" the structure of their beliefs.

Role Preferences

A second and more direct measure of the professional values of the Catholic college professor is the way he ranks his personal preferences among the role functions of an academic man. What aspects of his role attract his interest? How does he rank the other activities of an academician? Does he see himself as a teacher or as a research man or as a combination of both? And how about his views on the functionally necessary role of the academic administrator?

These questions focus attention on the self-image of the Catholic professor in terms which impute value orientations on a teaching-research continuum. They are not questions which can be easily answered, given the multiple functions and attractions of the academic role, nor are today's answers necessarily those of tomorrow. In addition, they are questions which are vulnerable to stereotype responses which cannot be properly tested for validity. The man who prefers to teach may have had research opportunities thrust upon him and he may have reluctantly exploited them. His research-minded colleague, on the other hand, may be frustrated because his opportunities for research have been so few or because he has had time only for his teaching or administrative duties.

The rank ordering of role preferences, therefore, is an uncertain tool. It suggests rather than establishes the structure of professional values, and even this in broad strokes. By itself it is a gross descriptive measure, but in combination with the orientations indicated in the value-conflict cases to follow, it provides a basis for outlining the value profile of the Catholic academic man.[2]

The self-image of the Catholic professor expressed in role-preference terms is first and foremost that of a teacher. The data of Table 12 clearly establish this bias on the part of more than

Table 12.—Distribution of Catholic Academicians
by Rank Ordering of Role Preferences
(Percentages)

Role Preferences	Rank Order of Preference			
	1	2	3	4
Undergraduate teaching	57.3	20.2	15.4	3.0
Graduate teaching	22.9	37.8	25.1	7.9
Research	12.4	23.6	41.9	15.7
Academic administration	3.4	12.4	11.2	67.0
No choice	4.0	6.0	6.4	6.4
TOTALS	100.0	100.0	100.0	100.0

80% of the faculty. Over 57% identified the undergraduate level of instruction as their first preference, but another 22% were primarily attracted to teaching at the graduate level. The former were more often priests than laymen and more often non-Ph.D.'s on the staffs of smaller colleges; while the latter tended to be lay Ph.D.'s at larger institutions. These internal differences, however, are less significant than the dominant preference expressed for the teaching sub-role at whatever level.

Against the background data of earlier chapters, this clear-cut preference for teaching over research and administration is not unexpected. But the devaluation of the research and administrative functions of the academic role is even more conspicuous than predicted. The low estate of academic administration is a professional commonplace, but the special situation of Catholic academicians has probably accentuated it. This appears in the fact that only one priest and eight laymen made it their first choice. Over two-thirds of the faculty, on the other hand, ranked administration last, and many emphasized their personal antipathy to such an assignment by suggesting that "104" or "infinity" be used to describe its ranking. The general non-eligibility of the lay professors for the higher administrative positions, and the fact that these posts are not defined as rewards by the religious, are significant factors here.

The ranking of the research functions of the academic role presents a more complex picture. As a first choice it attracted the preference of only 12.4% of the Catholic academicians and was clearly less valued than teaching. A more positive picture of the values placed upon research emerges, however, when it is seen that 36% identify it as a first *or* second choice.

The interview materials suggested that some professors were interested in the research functions of their roles but that, in the context of their personal and institutional situations, it had to be ranked below teaching. Others were so completely committed to the teaching sub-roles or so unsympathetic to the research function that their problem was one of weighing the "evils" of research and administration. The differences in the ranking of research by the religious and lay professors are here particularly interesting. In rank order of preference, the priests ranked research as first choice (7%), second choice (30%), third choice (51%), fourth choice (12%). The lay professors chose research as their first role preference in 16% of the cases or more than twice as frequently as the priests, but they also had a larger proportion (20%) locating research as a last choice. The 23% and 41% respectively who ranked research as a second or third choice are not significantly different from their religious colleagues.

The value implications of these rank orderings of the Catholic academicians' role preferences cannot be directly and simply inferred from the statistics. The question forced them to make hair-line decisions, to split functions which are often closely related, and to evaluate some activities with which they had no personal experience. Moreover, the difficulties of interpretation were compounded by the double opportunity to indicate a teaching preference (graduate and undergraduate) and by the irrelevance of administration to the career images of so many professors.

As a consequence, the statistical summary of their role preferences tends to emphasize the extremes and to obscure the often-mixed role preferences of the faculty members. For these reasons the respondent's ranking of research is here used as the basis for constructing a sub-profile of professional value-orientations based on role preferences. Thus, those ranking research as a first preference were classified as research-oriented, those ranking it second were classified as neutral or mixed in orientation, those classifying it as third choice were identified as teaching-oriented. Administrative role preferences were eliminated.

Figure A

Value-Orientation Sub-Profile of Catholic
Academicians Based on Role Preferences
(Percentages)

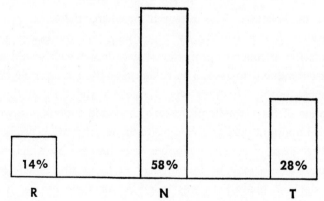

| 14% | 58% | 28% |
| R | N | T |

Figure A describes the value-orientation sub-profile which emerges from this use of research preferences as a discriminating index. Two facts are immediately conspicuous. First, the neutral or mixed orientation category (58%) comprises the largest single value grouping. Second, the distribution of value orientations is surprisingly proportionate, with the research-oriented group (14%) being only half as large as the teaching-oriented (28%), and this in turn being only slightly less than half the proportion of the neutral or mixed orientation group (58%). At this point the composition of each category and the social factors relevant to its respective value orientations will not concern us. These points will be raised later when the sub-profile drawn by role preferences is combined with a second sub-profile of value orientation based on different measures.

Value-Conflict Decisions

As value-orientation indices, the role preferences of the Catholic academic men are suggestive but incomplete. They point the directions of professional values, but their reliability as indices may be suspect because they express self-images and because they may be projections of stereotypes rather than functional bases of behavior. The research problem, therefore, was to neutralize this possibility by identifying the professor's value orientation in concrete professional situations which would elicit clear-cut value responses. The value-orientation sub-profile based on such testing situations would sharpen and deepen the description of the Catholic professor's academic outlook and would be an important part of a composite value orientation profile.

There exist, of course, a number of techniques by which occupational values may be investigated at these situational levels. The decision made here was to probe for them by the use of problem cases, each structured to indicate a value orientation towards either research or teaching. Moreover, some degree of the commitment to either professional value was further investigated by having a "probable" or "definite" decision permitted in each case. The limited number and range of situations covered by these value-conflict cases qualify, of course, the extent and the accuracy with which they mirror the total structure of faculty values: in any event, they are useful as descriptive indicators of the values which are brought to *some* professional situations.

The following pages reproduce the six value-conflict cases on which each respondent was asked to make *one* decision. Accompanying each case there is a statistical table summarizing the distribution of decisions according to their hypothesized classification as a research-oriented or teaching-oriented resolution of the problem.

CASE A

Professor White was the Chairman of a faculty committee responsible for the nomination of a Senior for a highly prized graduate school scholarship. His colleagues were equally divided on the merits of the two top candidates. His decision, therefore, was going to be decisive.

Applicant C was a superior student who had maintained consistently high grades in all subjects. His work was described as being not too original but detailed, carefully organized, and well developed.

Applicant M was a superior student, but his grades were consistently high only in those courses in which he was interested. His work in these courses was described as highly creative and as displaying critical insight.

For whom should Professor White have voted?

(a) He definitely should have voted for C.   1
(b) He probably should have voted for C.   2
(c) He probably should have voted for M.   3
(d) He definitely should have voted for M.   4

Case A—Distribution of Decisions by Religious - Lay Status
and by Value-Orientation Hypotheses (Percentages)

Faculty Status	Orientation Hypothesized					
	Decision Circled					
	Teaching T		Research R			
	1	2	3	4	No. Ans.	Total
Religious	18.6	20.6	32.4	27.4	1.0	100.0
Lay	9.7	19.4	28.5	41.2	1.2	100.0
TOTAL	13.1	19.9	30.0	35.9	1.1	100.0

CASE B

Professor Smith was teaching in a college which stressed both
scholarship and teaching excellence in evaluating its faculty. A
publisher unexpectedly made him a firm offer to publish in book
form a revised and enlarged version of some research Smith had
completed. This revision and enlargement, however, involved
quite a bit of time. Smith had already been assigned a twelve-
credit-hour schedule which included two new courses. The
schedule could not be changed.

What should Professor Smith have done?

(a) He should have done a good job on the courses,
      even if the book had to wait a year.   1
(b) He should have done the book, even if the courses
      suffered in some degree.   2
(c) He should have done the book regardless of what
      happened to the courses.   3

Case B—Distribution of Decisions by Religious - Lay Status
and by Value-Orientation Hypotheses (Percentages)

Faculty Status	Orientation Hypothesized				
	Decision Circled				
	T 1	R 2	R 3	No. Ans.	Total
Religious	81.4	15.7	1.9	1.0	100.0
Lay	67.9	28.5	2.4	1.2	100.0
TOTAL	73.0	23.6	2.3	1.1	100.0

CASE C

Dr. Jones was a faculty member at a middle-sized college. For many reasons he was willing to consider a "change." Two colleges offered him appointments. Both were improvements on his situation. Both were located in acceptable regions and the salary provisions were approximately the same.

(a) *College X* was a fairly well-known college. It had some prominent scholars on its staff and its resources were limited, but it was "on the way up." Jones was offered appointment in the rank of Associate Professor. In two years he would receive tenure and he might become Department Chairman.

(b) *College Y* was quite well known. It had a distinguished faculty and extensive resources. Jones was offered a two-year appointment here in the rank of Assistant Professor. It was made clear to him that the renewal of his contract would depend on his scholarly productivity.

Which position should Jones have taken?

(a) He definitely should have taken the position at X. 1

(b) He probably should have taken the position at X.   2

(c) He probably should have taken the position at Y.   3

(d) He definitely should have taken the position at Y.   4

Case C—Distribution of Decisions by Religious - Lay Status
and by Value-Orientation Hypotheses (Percentages)

Faculty Status	Orientation Hypothesized					
	Decision Circled					
	T 1	T 2	R 3	R 4	No. Ans.	Total
Religious	19.6	21.6	33.3	22.5	3.0	100.0
Lay	21.8	38.8	25.5	12.7	1.2	100.0
TOTAL	21.0	32.2	28.5	16.5	1.8	100.0

CASE D

Professor Green was on the examination committee for a
doctoral candidate. During the examination it became clear
that this candidate did not meet his standards. It appeared that
the candidate, despite much hard work, had a rather limited
capacity in this field. Professor Green knew that the young man
had a wife and children and had been offered a position if he
passed the examination for his degree. Green also knew that the
institution which had offered to appoint the young candidate
had rather low standards and that, relative to the faculty there,
this candidate would not be the poorest in his field.

How should Professor Green have voted?

(a) He definitely should have voted to fail him.   1

(b) He probably should have voted to fail him.   2

(c) He probably should have voted to pass him.   3

(d) He definitely should have voted to pass him.   4

Case D—Distribution of Decisions by Religious - Lay Status and by Value-Orientation Hypotheses (Percentages)

Faculty Status	Orientation Hypothesized					
	Decision Circled					
	T 1	T 2	R 3	R 4	No. Ans.	Total
Religious	36.3	31.3	26.5	4.9	1.0	100.0
Lay	35.8	31.5	25.5	5.4	1.8	100.0
TOTAL	36.0	31.5	25.8	5.2	1.5	100.0

CASE E

Professor Black was a member of a fairly small but good department. Two men were being considered for appointment to a tenure position, but only one would be appointed. As a senior member of the department, Black's opinion was solicited.

Professor A was known to be well liked by both his students and his colleagues. He was an effective teacher and was extremely well-read in his own field and in other areas. It was quite clear, however, that he was never going to make a significant contribution to the field.

Professor B was known to be a bit of a "loner." He did not have any really close friends and only the better students seemed to get much from his courses. It was quite clear, however, that in the long run he was destined to be one of the intellectual leaders in his field.

Which man should Professor Black have recommended?

(a) He definitely should have recommended Prof. A.   1
(b) He probably should have recommended Prof. A.   2
(c) He probably should have recommended Prof. B.   3
(d) He definitely should have recommended Prof. B.   4

Case E—Distribution of Decisions by Religious - Lay Status
and by Value-Orientation Hypotheses (Percentages)

| Faculty Status | Orientation Hypothesized | | | | | |
| | Decision Circled | | | | | |
	T 1	T 2	R 3	R 4	No. Ans.	Total
Religious	43.2	24.5	18.6	12.7	1.0	100.0
Lay	29.7	29.7	23.0	15.8	1.8	100.0
TOTAL	34.8	27.7	21.4	14.6	1.5	100.0

CASE F

Professor Doe had been a member of a college faculty for some years. His Departmental Chairman and Dean were very satisfied with his work and he was under no pressure to publish. Unexpectedly, an opportunity was provided him to do some research which might make an important contribution to his field. If he undertook the research, he would have to travel extensively and to give up the time which he enjoyed spending with his wife and children. There was no extra pay.

What should Professor Doe have done?

(a) He definitely should have done the research.   1
(b) He probably should have done the research.   2
(c) He probably should not have done the research.   3
(d) He definitely should not have done the research.   4

For the majority of the faculty respondents, these value-conflict problems were the most "interesting" parts of the interview. Most accepted the cases in noncommital fashion and circled their decisions. An occasional laugh, or frown, or sound of perplexity suggested that some recognized the situation as familiar or stereotyped or as difficult to evaluate. Some, indeed,

Case F—Distribution of Decisions by Religious - Lay Status
and by Value-Orientation Hypotheses (Percentages)

| Faculty Status | Orientation Hypothesized | | | | | |
| | Decision Circled | | | | | |
	R 1	R 2	T 3	T 4	No. Ans.	Total
Religious	41.2	38.2	12.7	5.9	2.0	100.0
Lay	41.8	40.0	12.2	4.2	1.8	100.0
TOTAL	41.6	39.3	12.3	4.9	1.9	100.0

commented on their own experiences or "talked out" their decision to themselves.

Among others, there were evidences of resistance to the assignment of deciding the value conflict. Typically, these professors questioned the adequacy or the importance of the information provided or, especially among the religious members, raised the question of moral issues perceived as present. This latter reaction was especially common as a frame of reference for resolving the conflict of the professor caught between the opportunity to publish his research and his assigned teaching obligations (Case B). His "moral" obligations to live up to his contract and to fulfill his responsibilities as a teacher were conspicuous notes of faculty reaction.

Similarly, some of the religious respondents were quite diffident about those problems which were outside their personal frames of reference. They indicated, for example, some comic relief at being outside the problem of the professor whose research would separate him from his wife and children (Case F), and they were somewhat less involved, or so it seemed, in the personal rewards contingent on publication (Case C). Like their lay colleagues, however, they "decided" almost every case and provided an empiric basis for projecting a value-orientation sub-profile.

Table 13 provides a grand summary of these value-conflict decisions according to the hypothesized value orientation, and the lay and religious status, of the respondents. Examined as a group of decisions, the most conspicuous pattern is the generally even distribution of the faculty decisions between the values hypothesized as conflicting. Thus, in Cases A, C, D, and E, the proportions "deciding" the conflict in research- and teaching-orientation terms range between 68% and 31% of the respondents. Only Case F (the research vs. family problem) and, to a lesser degree, Case B (publish or teach problem) appear to pose less significant value-conflict problems for the Catholic academic men. In these cases 81% and 74% share the same general value orientation, the former in the direction of approving a research decision, the latter in the direction of a teaching decision. Apart from these offsetting, "weaker" cases, the proportionate distribution of research-oriented and teaching-oriented decisions, and the distribution of their intensity as "probable" and "definite," suggest that the value-problem character of the test situations was empirically recognized and confirmed.

The construction of a value-orientation sub-profile from these faculty decisions involves (a) specifying the decisions which were hypothesized as indicating a research or a teaching orientation; and (b) establishing a formula which would locate each respondent on a continuum ranging from polar research to polar teaching orientations.

Table 13 has already indicated the decisions defined as expressing a research or teaching orientation. The formula for locating the "score" of each respondent sought to take into account the limited information provided in each case and the

Table 13.—Grand Summary Distribution of Catholic Religious and Lay Academicians by Conflict Decisions According to Hypothesized Research and Teaching Value-Orientations (Percentages)

Decisions	Case A				Case B				Case C				Case D				Case E				Case F			
	Hyp.	Rel.	Lay	Tot.	Hyp.	Rel.	Lay	Tot.	Hyp.	Rel.	Lay	Tot.	Hyp.	Rel.	Lay	Tot.	Hyp.	Rel.	Lay	Tot.	Hyp.	Rel.	Lay	Tot.
1	T	19	10	13	T	82	69	74	T	20	22	21	T	37	36	36	T	43	30	35	R	41	42	42
2	T	21	20	20	R	16	29	24	T	22	39	33	T	32	32	32	T	39	30	28	R	38	41	39
3	R	32	29	30	R	2	2	2	R	34	26	29	R	27	26	26	R	13	23	21	T	13	12	12
4	R	28	41	36	—	—	—	—	R	23	13	17	R	5	5	5	R	6	16	15	T	6	4	5

varieties of faculty experiences and situations. No distinction was made, therefore, between "probable" and "definite" decisions. Professors who decided in either degree in the direction of the assumed research value-position in all six or in any five of the cases were grouped as a research-oriented pole (RR). Similarly, a total of any four research and any two teaching value-decisions resulted in an intermediate classification (RI) relative to the polar research group and to the neutral group (N) who were so scored if they made three research decisions and three teaching decisions. Conversely, we have an intermediate classification (IT) relative to the polar teaching group (TT). This design lessens the critical significance of decisions made by the faculty in as many as two cases and partially compensates for the differences in the discriminatory value of the limited number of cases.

Figure B describes the proportionate distribution of these conflict-decision-based value orientations.

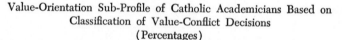

Figure B

Value-Orientation Sub-Profile of Catholic Academicians Based on
Classification of Value-Conflict Decisions
(Percentages)

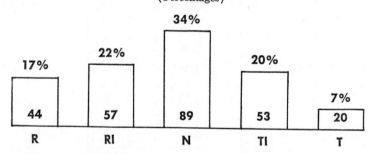

The most striking feature of this sub-profile is the proportionately larger representation of Catholic professors in the research-oriented categories. Compared to the 14% located in this value-orientation category in the role-preferences sub-profile, 17% are here identified as deciding the problem cases in favor of research values in at least five of the six cases, while another 22% did so in four of the cases. The combined proportion of research-oriented professors (39%) is the largest single value-orientation grouping. A comparison of the proportions, not of the professors, in the two sub-profiles suggests that the research-oriented category grew in the conflict-decisions measure at the expense of the neutral or mixed category. This declined from 58% in the role-preferences sub-profile to 33% here. The proportions of those in the teaching-oriented categories, however, remained almost unchanged (28% in the role-preference measure and 27% in the value-conflict cases).

The increase in the proportion of those indicating a research value-orientation is open to many interpretations. It may reflect the biases of the test cases or the attraction of stereotypes which endorse and recommend research-oriented decisions. Again, it may only mean that the hypotheses by which the decisions were classified as research- or teaching-oriented were at least partly ambiguous. But the shift to research-oriented decisions may also mean that, independent of personal role preferences, viable research value-orientations may be present and may find expression in concrete problem-cases. More than anything else, the differences in the sub-profiles confirm the complexity of the professional perceptions which are present within the same academic person and within the academic group.

THE COMPOSITE VALUE-ORIENTATION PROFILE

The value orientation sub-profiles of the Catholic academician derived from these role preference- and conflict-decision measures are, in their present form, mainly of descriptive value. Each has sketched in the grosser parts of a value-orientation profile, but in the process they have obscured the uniqueness of the professional perspectives of the individual professor. Is Professor X really interested in research, as he says he is, or is he, in fact, more teaching-oriented? Is Father Y, on the other hand, more sympathetic to research values than he's willing to admit? And is Professor Z really as confused and uncertain about his role as he seems to be? These questions focus on the individual professor and on the particular combinations of his responses to the value-orientation measures. The structural similarities or differences and the number of these individual composites provide a basis for drawing the sociological profile of the composite value orientations of the Catholic academic group.

The procedure used here is quite simple. A composite value-orientation profile was constructed for each professor based upon the pattern of his responses to the role-preference and conflict-decision measures. The analysis of these individual value-orientation profiles identified four fairly distinct groupings of faculty responses. These are: (1) the research-oriented category, professors who were research-oriented in role preferences and in at least four value-conflict cases; (2) the neutral- or dual-value-oriented, composed of respondents who were neutral in role preference and who made three research-oriented and three teaching-oriented value-conflict decisions; (3) the teaching-oriented category, composed of academicians who were teaching-oriented in role preference and in at least four value-conflict cases; (4) the ambivalent category of those professors who were research-oriented in one measure and teaching-oriented in the other. Figure C describes this composite value-orientation profile of the Catholic academic man and the proportionate distribution of the faculty respondents in each category.

The most conspicuous feature of this profile is the identification of 46% of the Catholic college faculty as teaching-oriented in

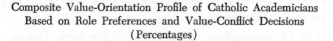

Figure C

Composite Value-Orientation Profile of Catholic Academicians
Based on Role Preferences and Value-Conflict Decisions
(Percentages)

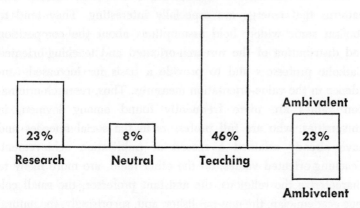

their professional values. This proportion is twice as large as that attracted to the opposite, or research-oriented, pole (23%). Equally significant is the evidence that a like proportion (23%) are, by these measures at least, ambivalent with regard to their research and teaching perspectives, while only 8% are neutral, or dual-oriented, in their value positions. The absence of comparable value-orientation data for non-Catholic professors is, of course, a major handicap to analysis. It can only be said that the general structure of the composite profile corresponds to what might have been predicted on the basis of the life history data of the Catholic professors.

Two questions concerning this value-orientation profile of the Catholic academic man remain to be answered. Who are the professors in each value category? What are the social sources or factors related to their respective value orientations? This latter question will occupy our attention in the following part of this chapter. Here some of the descriptive and analytically significant dimensions of the profile will be provided by detailing the composition of each value-orientation group in terms of present professional statuses.

Table 14 summarizes the details of five such factors. The patterns that emerge are especially interesting. They tend to confirm some widely held assumptions about the composition and distribution of the research-oriented and teaching-oriented Catholic professors and to provide a basis for increased confidence in the value-orientation measures. Thus, research-orientation values are more frequently found among laymen, in universities, who are full professors in the social sciences and have already attained a record of publication achievement. Teaching-oriented values, on the other hand, are more likely to characterize the religious, the assistant professor, the small college academician, the non-publisher, and, surprisingly, the natural scientist. Significantly, the ambivalent faculty members tend to be drawn in the greater proportions from those who are associate professors in the humanities divisions of middle-sized colleges.

Except for the low representation of the sample's natural scientists in the research-oriented category, these distributions follow the expected patterns. Relatively few of the differences, it is true, are statistically large, but given the two-to-one ratio of teaching-oriented to research-oriented professors, they are significant clues to the structure and distribution of these professional values among Catholic academicians.

WHY?

At this point the question arises as to why these different groups of Catholic professors are attracted to their respective value orientations. Why are so many of them teaching-oriented and so relatively few research-oriented? Why, too, are so many

Table 14.—Distribution of Catholic Academicians' Value Orientations by Religious - Lay Status, Rank, Size of Institution, Academic Area and Publication Index (Percentages)

Value Orientations		Status		Rank				Size of Institution			Academic Area			Publication Index		
		Rel.	Lay	Prof.	Assoc. Prof.	Asst. Prof.	Inst.	L	M	S	Humanities	Natural Science	Social Science	4.3	2	1.0
R	(57)	17	27	32	21	14	25	26	18	24	19	17	31	30	22	23
M	(21)	11	5	6	4	15	13	6	12	8	7	18	4	11	9	10
T	(117)	50	45	38	47	56	47	45	41	56	46	47	47	36	44	48
RT	(56)	22	23	24	28	15	15	23	29	12	28	18	18	23	25	19
Total	(251)	100	100	100	100	100	100	100	100	100	100	100	100	100	100	100

ambivalent in their professional outlook with regard to these value dimensions?

The answers to these questions are necessarily limited by the quantity and quality of the research materials. We will not attempt to explain why Professor X perceives his role in one way while Professor Y sees *his* in quite another. The complexity of each case, and the different significance of even the same factor for different professors, make such analysis impossible.

The focus, rather, is on the group who share with Professor X the same value orientation. It is hypothesized that those who share a common value orientation will have shared, too, a similar set of socializing experiences in their formative years. Whether or not these experiences have functioned in the predicted fashion, or whether they have been neutralized or even reversed in their effects by other significant socializing experiences, cannot be here determined for individual cases. The statistical premise is that each orientation group will reveal certain distinctive differences in the proportionate distribution of key socializing influences. It is further assumed that the patterning of these differences points to "their functional significance" in the development of the various value orientations. In a word, they are "clues" as to why some professors are oriented to research values while others are teaching-oriented or ambivalent.

The two broad sets of socializing influences against which the various value-orientation groups are here studied are the family and the school. Each available research fact in these areas was defined as an independent variable for purposes of analysis. The following sections describe only those variables in which differences of some theoretical and statistical significance appeared. The absence of such differences in the many other factors examined may be interpreted as indicating their lesser significance as socializing forces or their greater vulnerability to neutralization or change by other, later or non-investigated factors. Conversely the persisting significance of the factors that discriminate the value-orientation groups is a research warrant for their more detailed analysis.

Professional Values and Family Socialization

When the distribution of each family background factor is compared to the proportionate representation of the Catholic professors in the various composite value-orientation groups, only a few socializing influences emerge in ratios other than those of a binomial distribution. There is no significant difference, for example, in the proportions who were reared in large cities and the distribution of value-orientation groups. Such factors, therefore, do not appear to have been significant influences in the formation of value perspectives.

Tables 15 and 16 identify respectively the environmental and psycho-social factors in the Catholic academicians' family socialization which "make a difference." These data indicate that socialization in the direction of research values is more likely when the professor's father had himself experienced higher education and was a professional person or a farmer. Conversely, those whose fathers had no more than high school education and were service workers were least likely to be research-oriented and most likely to express teaching-oriented values. These facts are especially important because they relate the low proportion of research-oriented Catholic professors to the type of family-based environments which are the rule rather than the exception in their life histories. This is certainly not a new observation, but the prominence of non-research values among Catholic academicians is seen empirically to be at least partly grounded in the lower socio-economic environments of their early socialization.

An even more dramatic source of this dominant teaching

Table 15.—Distribution of Catholic Academicians' Value Orientations by Education of Father and Occupation of Father (Percentages)

Composite Value Orientation	Education of Father		Occupation of Father								
	Non-College	College	Prof.	Mgr.	Clerical	Sales	Crafts-man	Operation	Service	Lab.	Farmer
R (56)	21.3	27.0	34.6	20.0	25.0	18.5	19.5	25.0	15.0	18.5	33.3
M (21)	8.8	9.6	3.8	5.4	12.5	11.1	12.2	8.3	15.0	7.4	11.1
T (113)	47.2	42.4	38.5	47.3	37.5	66.6	31.7	58.4	60.0	44.4	33.3
RT (56)	22.7	21.0	23.1	27.3	25.0	3.8	36.6	8.3	10.0	29.7	22.3
Total (246)	100.0	100.0	100.0	100.0	100.0	100.0	100.0	100.0	100.0	100.0	100.0

Table 16.—Distribution of Catholic Academicians' Value Orientations by Father's Religion, Religious Climate of Family, Parental Authority, Parental Supervision, and Affective Ties to Parents (Percentages)

Value Orientations	Father's Religion			Religious Climate of Family				Parental Authority			Parental Supervision					Affective Ties to Parents					
	R.C.	Prot.	Other Non-Catholic	Strong	Average	Not Strong	No Ans.	Father Authority Figure	Equal Authority	Mother Authority Figure	Strict	Fairly Strict	Same as Others	Some Freedom	Much Freedom	Closer to Father	Equal	Closer to Mother	Not Close	Cannot Answer	No Ans.
R	20	40	39	17	29	30	33	21	24	22	21	15	8	16	43	20	23	21	33	21	—
M	9	8	8	10	6	9	—	8	13	9	8	8	25	13	2	4	9	9	10	7	—
T	47	33	39	49	42	48	67	43	43	53	46	45	67	54	38	64	49	43	33	50	100
RT	24	19	14	24	23	13	—	28	20	16	25	32	—	17	17	12	19	27	24	22	—
Tot.	100	100	100	100	100	100	100	100	100	100	100	100	100	100	100	100	100	100	100	100	100

orientation is identified in Table 16. The evidence here points to the fact that non-research values have been nurtured in those families which were at once "Catholic" and "strongly religious" and in which the childhood years of the professor were not marked by much personal freedom of action and decision. Thus, 40% of the respondents whose fathers were Protestant have a research-oriented value orientation compared to 20% of those whose fathers were Catholic. The importance of the Protestant father's influence in this direction is, moreover, somewhat special because there is no appreciable difference here in the research-oriented influences of Protestant and Catholic mothers. Indeed, the former are, in somewhat greater proportion, represented by professor-sons with a teaching value-orientation.

Especially interesting, too, are the patterns which relate the "strongly religious" family environment to minimal representation in the research-oriented category (17.4%) and to the higher proportions respectively of teaching-oriented (48.6%) and am-bivalent (24.3%) professors. This pattern is in sharp contrast to the value-orientation proportions of those socialized in a "religiously weak" family. Almost as large a ratio, it is true, are teaching-oriented, but the research-oriented and ambivalent proportions of 30.4% and 13.1% are approximately twice as large and twice as small respectively as those from "strongly religious" families.

This evidence clearly suggests that the non-research value profile of the Catholic academic man is a more or less direct consequence of religiously perceived influences. Our imperfect knowledge of the ethnic origins of the faculty makes impossible any more precise weighting of the religious factor in the formation of these professional values. It would appear, however, that the configuration which identifies a "Catholic" family socialization and a "strongly religious" family climate with non-research values cannot be denied analytical significance. As experienced by the majority of the Catholic professors, these religious influences have inhibited the development of research values and have fostered a teaching orientation.

An order of evidence positively related to this interpretation is seen in the description of the Catholic academician's affective and authority relationships to his parents. As Table 16 indicates, the proportion who are research-oriented tends to be unaffected by the possible differences in the parental authority-figure. But where the professors' mothers tended to be, or definitely were, the family heads, the teaching orientation was more frequently found; when the father was the family authority-figure, a greater proportion were ambivalent as to research and teaching values.

Who the authority-figure was, however, turns out to be less of a clue to the development of value orientations than the degree of authority experienced. This is proved by the clear-cut patterns that relate a strictly supervised childhood to teaching values and to ambivalent perspectives, while those who experienced much freedom during these years are more likely to emphasize a research orientation.[3] These relationships tend to confirm not only the much-reported Catholic bias in favor of authoritarian family structures but the dysfunctional consequences of non-freedom in terms of individual and creative achievements.

The impressive consistency with which these environmental and psycho-social aspects of family socialization "explain" the value orientations of Catholic professors cannot be ignored. At the same time the variants—those cases in which the unpredicted value perspective appears—can not be simply glossed over. Whether or not the people in these cases have developed their professional values because of, or in spite of, their family socialization, or as the result of later or even uninvestigated influences cannot be readily determined. The "clues" provided by the research findings need further and more detailed study.

Professional Values and School Socialization

The relationships between the type of schooling experienced by the Catholic professors and their composite value orientations also provide important analytical clues. Table 17 summarizes these data. Perhaps the most interesting finding is the change from the pre-college to college levels in the type of value orientations characteristic of professors educated in Catholic and non-Catholic schools. In the pre-college period, the differences in this respect between parochial and public school education are not large. The data describe the Catholic school graduate as somewhat more research-oriented and somewhat less teaching-oriented than his colleagues from a public school background: for example, 25.2% of those from Catholic high schools were research-oriented compared to 17.3% of those from public secondary schools.

The critical question is, what happened in Catholic colleges and graduate schools? Our data provide no ready answer. Table 17 clearly indicates, however, that the professors who earned their Bachelor's and Master's degrees in Catholic institutions were in larger proportions least likely to be research-oriented and most likely to be teaching-oriented. Moreover, the differences between the Catholic and non-Catholic college graduates in these orientations increase with the level of their degree attainments except for those with a Ph.D. Only 20% of those with Bachelor's and Master's degrees from Catholic colleges are in the research-oriented category compared to 33.3% and 30.0% of their colleagues holding degrees from non-Catholic institutions.

This disproportion becomes even greater when the Catholic and non-Catholic settings of all graduate study (including that being done by faculty members who are still degree candidates) are compared. The research value-orientation is associated with

Table 17.—Distribution of Catholic Academicians' Value Orientations by Type of School Attended at All Educational Levels (Percentages)

Composite Value Orientation	Elementary School		Secondary School		College		Master's		Ph.D.	
	Catholic Only	Public Only	Catholic Only	Public Only	Catholic Only	Non-Cath. Only	Catholic Only	Non-Cath. Only	Catholic Only	Non-Cath. Only
R	22.3	19.7	25.2	17.3	20.4	33.3	20.6	30.0	29.4	29.8
M	11.5	3.9	9.5	8.0	8.4	6.7	8.1	4.0	10.2	8.8
T	43.1	51.3	42.8	50.6	47.6	37.7	46.3	41.4	40.8	40.4
RT	23.1	25.1	22.5	24.1	23.6	22.3	25.0	24.6	19.6	21.0
Totals	100.0	100.0	100.0	100.0	100.0	100.0	100.0	100.0	100.0	100.0

only 10.6% of the Catholic graduate schools' products compared to 29.1% of those identified with non-Catholic graduate institutions. Moreover, over one-third of the Catholic graduate school alumni are ambivalent in their professional views of research and teaching, compared to 20.9% of their colleagues whose graduate education was received at non-Catholic universities. The only exception to this pattern of difference appears in the almost identical value-orientation distributions of the doctoral degree holders from Catholic and non-Catholic universities.

This relative depreciation of research values by Catholic professors educated in Catholic colleges and universities is not surprising. Until recent years these institutions were still largely outside the influence of the values developing in the dominant system of non-Catholic higher education. Their objectives, their professors, and their facilities were so out of tune with the research spirit that it could not be communicated or demonstrated by example. As students no less than as sons, the majority of the Catholic professors were socialized in institutional settings which endorsed values and behavior more congenial to the role of the teacher than to that of the research scholar.

Summary

The self-images of Catholic professors and the structure of their professional values and attitudes define them as teaching- rather than research-scholars. This is clearly established in the evidence that a majority of the sample identified each of five test statements as sources of teaching satisfaction, and in their ranking of the teaching sub-role significantly higher than research or administration. The teaching-oriented direction of these explicit measures of professional values was somewhat balanced by the decisions that many of the Catholic professors made in specific research-teaching conflict cases. Even here, however, the prominence of teaching- over research-values persists. The analysis of separate cases further reveals that, especially among the religious professors, moral considerations are significant sources of teaching- over research-preferences.

The reasons for these value orientations vary, of course, by individuals. Typically those who are teaching-oriented have internalized these values in distinctive family and school environments. Proportionately they have been socialized in strongly Catholic working-class families and in the exclusive contexts of Catholic elementary, secondary, and collegiate institutions. Their research-oriented colleagues, on the other hand, were more frequently the products of the different socialization influences of non-Catholic or more socially mobile Catholic families and, especially, of non-Catholic colleges and universities.

VII

THE PUBLISHING AND
THE NON-PUBLISHING PROFESSORS

Why do so few Catholic academic men publish the results of their scholarly thought and research? What factors distinguish the publishing and non-publishing sub-groups of the Catholic college faculty? These questions move the analysis of the professional status of the Catholic academician from the level of value orientation to that of academic performance.

The focus on the publication index of faculty performance is admittedly one-sided and incomplete. It neglects not only the importance of the teaching functions of the academic man but the significant differences in the quality of teaching performance. And this shortcoming is compounded by the fact that the publishing professors are distinguished from their non-publishing colleagues by the simple fact of publication and without reference to the quality of their work.

These deficiencies and their attendant problems are, of course, not unique to this study. They are the hardy annuals of faculty-administration debates for which no acceptable solution has been found. The focus on the publication index of faculty performance does not, therefore, deny the values and the differences in quality of the teaching or other sub-roles. It is used partly because the survey method provided little opportunity for investigating teaching performances and partly because the non-publication record of Catholic professors is an empiric fact of academic performance which distinguishes them from their non-Catholic colleagues.

The empiric evidence of Catholic college faculty non-publication needs no detailed restatement. It is established here in the fact that the publishing sub-sample numbers only 76 professors compared to 199 who have little or no record of publication. This latter group is composed of religious and lay professors who had individual publishing indices of 0, 1, or 2 and were all members of the randomly selected faculty sample. The publishing sub-group, on the other hand, was composed of 61 faculty members, similarly selected for inclusion in the study, and of 15 additional "elite" professors who were identified by their colleagues as "doing the best scholarly work" on their respective campuses.[1] The inclusion of this "elite" group positively skews the composition of the publishing sample since it reduced the disproportion in the size of the groups and provided a sharper base for the comparison of the publishing and non-publishing professors. All 76 members of this group had individual publishing indices of 3 or 4.

Table 18 sets the stage for the analysis of these faculty sub-samples by describing the composition of the publishing and non-publishing professors according to region, size of college, religious or lay status, and subject area. The most conspicuous fact is the high proportion of non-publishers within each of these categories. The minority who publish are laymen more often than religious, and natural scientists more often than social scientists or humanists. In addition, it appears that Catholic professors are

Table 18.—Distribution of Catholic Academic Men in Publishing and Non-Publishing Samples According to Region of College, Size of College, Religious - Lay Status, and Subject Areas
(Percentages)

Sub-Groups	Region of College				Size of College			Status		Subject Area		
	East (73)	Midwest (128)	South (38)	West (36)	L (114)	M (99)	S (62)	Rel. (108)	Lay (167)	Hum. (113)	N.S. (60)	S.S. (101)
Publishing (76)	22	32	27	25	36	28	11	24	30	26	32	28
Non-Publishing (199)	78	68	73	75	64	72	89	76	70	74	68	72
Totals (275)	100	100	100	100	100	100	100	100	100	100	100	100

somewhat more likely to publish if they are located in the Midwest and are on the staffs of the larger institutions.

The differences within each category, it should be noted, are seldom conspicuous, and their structures provide no real surprises. They confirm not only the suspected differences in publication orientation and publication opportunity by size of institution but also the Knapp and Greenbaum finding relative to the higher publication indices of Catholic natural scientists over social scientists and humanists.[2] The differences in the publication performance of the lay and religious professors also follows an expected pattern. Indeed the only unanticipated fact is the rank-order position of the faculty of Eastern institutions. The popular image of these institutions as older, larger, and better-known had provided a basis for expecting that the publishing proportion of their faculties would be larger than that of some other regions. The contradictory finding provides room for much speculation and debate—which, however, will not be entered upon here.

The comparative analysis of the factors distinguishing these publishing and non-publishing Catholic professors was guided by two general sets of assumptions. First, it was hypothesized that the publishing professors would be distinguished from their non-publishing colleagues by patterned differences in the values, motivations, and role models present to their respective socialization in their family and school environments. Secondly, it was hypothesized that the institutional setting in which the Catholic professors worked would be at least grossly significant to their publishing or non-publishing performance. Chapter VIII describes the research findings relevant to this latter assumption. The present chapter summarizes the relationships found between the publication or non-publication records of the faculty and their socialization in family and school environments.

PUBLICATION AND FAMILY SOCIALIZATION

The research materials on family background make it possible to analyze their publication or non-publication status in terms of two major types of socialization measures. The first of these concerns the grosser features of the family environment during childhood and adolescence; the second investigates the statistical relationship between their publication status and certain more specific features of family structure.

Family Environment

The analysis of the data describing the family environments clearly identifies one major publication handicap under which they have been laboring. Simply put, this handicap has been the generally low cultural environment of their parents' families as this is reflected in the educational and occupational attainments of the parents themselves. This is not a new or sufficient explanation of their non-publication record, but it does confirm in detail the validity of Ellis' and O'Dea's emphasis on the negative publication implications of such a family environment.[3]

The statistical facts identify by accumulation this environmental block to publication achievement. It is seen in the fact that, of the 45% of the professors' fathers who had been limited to elementary school education, only 26.9% of their sons were in the publishing sub-sample. By way of contrast 33.9% of those whose fathers had gone to college had publishing indices of 3 or 4. Indirectly, at least, these disproportions relate the non-publication of the majority of Catholic professors to an academically disadvantaged family environment.

The interpretation finds support in the structure of paternal occupations reported respectively by the publishing and non-publishing faculty respondents. In rank order, the former were more frequently the sons of service workers, professional persons, farmers and sales workers. Their non-publishing colleagues, on the other hand, were more often the sons of laborers, craftsmen, managers, and operative employees. As far as the overall publication record of the Catholic academicians is concerned, the significance of these patterns of relationship appears in the fact that the occupations of the fathers of the non-publishing professors constitute 58.2% of the total paternal occupations, while the occupations of the publishing professors represent 37.8% of the same total. By specific occupational category, the implications are illustrated in the finding that 39% of the sons of professional persons were in the publishing sub-sample compared to 14.3% of the sons of laborers.

The "neatness" of this positive relationship between publication performance and the higher-ranked paternal occupations is, however, upset by the evidence that 52% of the sons of service workers had publishing indices of 3 or 4. Whether this uniquely high relationship can be explained in terms of the influence of extrafamilial socialization forces, or in terms of a special performance-oriented emphasis associated with the paternal service employment, cannot be now determined. It remains a striking variation. It does not, however, invalidate the fact that for the majority of the Catholic academic men the occupationally inferred cultural environment of their families did not directly support the values and models positively associated with publication achievement.

Finally, and as a separate variable, the formal identification of the religious affiliation of the parents of the Catholic academicians is hypothetically relevant to publication performance. The data on this point indicate that while over 80% of the professors had two Catholic parents, this fact was negatively rather than positively associated with membership in the publishing sub-sample. Thus, compared to the 26% whose parents were both Catholics, and who had publishing indices of 3 or 4, similar indices of publication were reported by 35% of those whose fathers were non-Catholic and by 40% of those whose mothers were non-Catholic.[4] These gross patterns confirm the findings of Lenski, Rosen, McClelland and others which correlate positive attachment to the achievement syndrome with non-Catholic rather than with Catholic socialization experiences.[5] They indirectly support, too, O'Dea's thesis concerning the intellectually inhibiting characteristics of the dominant socio-religious values and processes of American Catholic life.[6]

In sum, the minority of the Catholic professors who have quantitatively impressive publishing records appear to have been the beneficiaries of family environments marked by the higher educational attainments of their fathers, by generally higher levels of paternal occupation, and, relative to their proportional representations in the sample, by the socialization influences of a non-Catholic parent. The non-publishing majority, on the other hand, seem to have been placed at a disadvantage: their family environments were less characterized by the influence of high parental educational and occupational attainments and were more frequently and more totally Catholic in religious tone. No single factor is a dramatic discriminator of the publishing and non-publishing professors; but the configurations of parental education, occupation, and religion are clearly related to each type of academic performance.

Family Structures

On a more direct and personal level, the publication and non-publication records of the Catholic academic men were also found to be related to the structure of parental values and parent-son relationships. The nature of these socializing influences was described by the respondents in the interviews and has been organized for statistical analysis in order to investigate the connections between such fundamental personality-forming influences and the publication performance of the Catholic college faculty. Again it should be noted that these data describe statistical patterns of relationship. In individual cases, publication and non-publication may have resulted in spite of, rather than because of, these influences.

Against the background of numerous studies which have identified the generally authoritarian structure of Catholic family life,[7] it is not surprising to find that 66% of the Catholic professors describe their boyhood as closely supervised by one or both parents. Indeed, 50% considered their parents' supervision as "strict" and only 30% reported that they enjoyed relative or extended freedom. The critical fact is that the proportion of those describing their parents as strict was lower (24%) in the publishing sub-sample than that of the other four discipline categories. The differences, it should be noted, are not statistically large. Nevertheless the negative direction of this relationship in publication terms and the dominance of this type of parental authority among Catholic academicians are analytically significant facts. They tend to confirm the dysfunctional consequences of authoritarian socialization experiences, as far as achievement orientation and performance are concerned, as reported by Lenski, McClelland, and others.[8] They suggest that the family socialization structure in which the majority of the Catholic professors were reared rewarded dependency and obedience and ill-prepared its sons for the critical, individualistic, independent requirements of scholarly research and publication.

The non-achievement, non-publication direction of the family socialization structure is indicated, too, by the data describing the parental authority-figure in each family. The majority of the faculty identified this figure as the father, but in terms which acknowledged, too, the importance of maternal authority. Thus, less than 10% identified their fathers as "definitely" the head of the family, while almost 45% described him as "tending" to be the head of the family—but with their mothers having a significant supporting authority role. In the remaining instances, the mother was described as either sharing the family authority equally, or as the dominant personality.

In terms of publication performance these differences in the authority-figure are again analytically interesting. The fact that 42% of those whose fathers were definitely the family head were included in the publishing sub-sample stands in sharp contrast to the evidence that 25.6% and 21.6% respectively of those whose fathers or mothers "tended" to be the family head were so located. This pattern suggests, as does Henry's study of the successful business man, that achievement orientation and motivation are more positively associated with paternal role models and paternal authority figures.[9] The relative absence of such clear-cut paternal authority in the families of the Catholic academic men, and the prominence instead of ambiguous or maternal authority-figures, are additional sources for explaining the low estate of Catholic college professors' publication records.

The non-publication significance of this ambiguous or maternal authority situation is reinforced by the patterns of affective ties to parents. Almost 50% of the faculty reported that they "felt closer" to their mothers when they were children while only 7.3% "felt closer" to their fathers. Whether or not this is an atypical pattern of parental preference is here irrelevant. The publication performance facts are that high indices of 3 or 4 were reported by 40% of those who "felt closer" to their fathers, by 31.6% of those who did not feel close to either parent, and by 24.3% of those who "felt closer" to their mothers. As before, the relatively lesser prominence of the masculine role model in the family socialization experiences of the majority of the Catholic faculty appears to have deprived them of the opportunity to internalize the values and attitudes required for achievement in the form of publication.

Finally, the research materials also indicate that the non-publication of Catholic faculty members is related to the uncertain prospects of higher education which marked their childhood and to the non-cultural perceptions of their parents toward education. The publishing professors proportionately come from families in which it was pretty much assumed that they would go to college.

Even more dramatically significant, however, are the data that indicate not only the prominence of a pragmatic, job-value, view of education on the part of the professors' parents, but also the negative consequences of this view in terms of the publication records of their sons. On the other hand, those whose parents were described as perceiving education primarily as a cultural value had publishing indices of 3 or 4 in over 40% of the cases. Again, the evidence is quite clear that the non-publication status of Catholic professors is, in significant measure, a product of family environments and family structures and values which constituted non-intellectual and non-achievement syndromes.

PUBLICATION AND SCHOOL SOCIALIZATION

For the academic man, the socialization experiences and influences of the school have a unique and direct career relevance. Indeed, few other occupations provide their recruits with so long and detailed and intimate a view of their work culture and worker roles. Prior to their training in medical schools, for example, few doctors have had much direct exposure to the professional work world of the office, clinic, or hospital. And the same is typically true for the lawyer, clergyman, etc. By way of contrast, the professor literally grows up in the environment of his work culture. Except for the reversal of roles, his professional career is an extension of an almost life-long formal involvement in the pursuit of knowledge. His teachers at every level and in every course provide him with role models, and the classroom, the library, and the laboratory are familiar work settings. To a unique degree, therefore, the career directions and career achievements of the academic man are functionally related to the socialization forces of his student years.

In their details, the relationships between these school socialization forces and the publication or non-publication performance of Catholic professors are not readily or easily subject to analysis. Again the relationship is not only mediated by the influence of extra-school factors; it is complicated by individual variations in the impact of even the same institutional setting and the same role models on the formation of career perspectives. Professor X, for example, may have inspired some of his students in the direction of research and publication. He may have just as decisively killed off such interests among others. Moreover, given the number of teacher models to which each professor has been exposed, the problem of identifying and weighing even the conscious sources of influence on publication performance outstripped the resources of the study. Here, therefore, it is only possible to investigate the relationships between publication or non-publication in terms of (a) the types of educational institution attended, and (b) academic achievements, career plans, and pre-professional situations.

Pre-College Education

To the popular controversy on the respective academic merits of parochial and public school elementary education, the publication performance of Catholic professors who attended each type of school provides no useful answer. The majority received their elementary schooling in Church-sponsored institutions, but this socialization fact seems to have no significant relationship to their publishing or non-publishing status. This conclusion is indicated by the research evidence that the publishing sub-sample included 27.4% of all those who had attended only parochial schools and 29.0% of those who had attended public schools. At this level, therefore, and on this measure, the situation is a standoff. It does not mean that differences in the socialization environment of parochial and public schools are nonexistent or are unrelated to the internalization of values and attitudes significant to other dimensions of the academic role. There is simply no research evidence that such differences are related to publication performance.

This undifferentiated picture changes, however, at the secondary or high school level. The research data here identify 32% of the sample's public high school alumni as publishing professors, compared to 21% of those graduated from parochial high schools. This difference, especially in the light of the college data below, cannot be dismissed as the result of chance or as insignificant. On the contrary, it dramatically spells out some of the personality and career consequences of the values, attitudes, and pattern of behavior learned in parochial as compared to public schools.

The non-statistical evidence of the interviews clearly indicates that the moral concerns of the religious teachers in Catholic secondary schools often got in the way of the development of achievement-oriented values. By word and act they modeled values of docility and obedience, attitudes of dependence and passivity, and behavior at once incurious and uncommitted as to intellectual activity. They "gave a lot of homework," but too often they failed to challenge the intellect and to stimulate the independent and critical pursuit of truth.

These socialization forces were not absent, of course, in the public school system, but there they were neutralized by the more functionally specific professional expectations institutionalized for the school and its teachers. The public school teacher could be challenged with relative impunity and could be discharged for unsatisfactory performance. The religious teacher in the parochial school generally could not be.

Finally, during this pre-college phase of their school socialization, the publishing and non-publishing directions of the Catholic professors' academic careers are previsioned by their scholastic ranking and by their career aspirations. The majority (66% in elementary school and 53% in high school) ranked themselves in the top ten percent of their classes. Compared to those with less impressive academic records, these superior students were somewhat more frequently found in the publishing sub-group.

But this unsurprising fact is less significant than the evidence that 70% and 66% of these superior students in elementary school and high school were not effectively socialized in the direction of publishing performance. If their academic records properly describe the Catholic professors' scholastic ability and industry at these points in their education, the intellectual potential for research and publication which was underdeveloped in school stands as a serious educational indictment.

The materials below clearly indicate that the college and career experiences of the majority compounded the non-publication socialization. On the side of the colleges, however, it should be pointed out that the Catholic professors' first "intellectual wasteland" was his elementary and secondary school education.

At this period, too, the direction of a publication or non-publication academic career appears to be related to the Catholic professors' career aspirations. Predictably, almost 50% of those identifying career plans by the end of their high school education (79% of the sample) were aspiring to the priesthood. The interesting fact is that this direction of their thinking and, no doubt, of their later experiences seems to have lessened the likelihood of their inclusion in the publishing sub-group. This is reflected in the evidence that 23% of those professors aspiring to the priesthood at that time had publishing indices of 3 or 4 compared to 34% of those identifying other occupations. By separate occupation the numbers are too small for any reliable correlation, but it is not without value to note that the publishing professors included 58% of those planning to become lawyers, 44% of those planning a teaching career, 41% of those thinking of medicine, and 40% of those interested in business.

This evidence of a selective relationship between occupational preferences and later publication achievement is open to multiple interpretations. Here it is enough to note that compared to specific secular professions, either the image of the priesthood or the type of person attracted to the priesthood is, at this point, less likely to be identified with strong achievement orientations.

College and University

On the basis of school environment, the most clear-cut discriminator between publishing and non-publishing performance is the type and level of higher education experienced by the faculty. Table 19 establishes one aspect of this in identifying the non-Catholic college graduates (43%) as publishing professors

Table 19.—Proportions of Catholic Professors in Publishing and Non-Publishing Sub-Groups by Catholic or Non-Catholic Institutional Sources of Bachelor's, Master's, and Doctoral Degrees (Percentages)

Sub-Group	Source of A.B., B.S. Degrees		Source of M.S., M.A. Degrees		Source of Ph.D.	
	Catholic College (210)	Non-Catholic College (54)	Catholic University (164)	Non-Catholic University (85)	Catholic University (59)	Non-Catholic University (66)
Publishing (76)	21	43	26	38	46	64
Non-Publishing (199)	79	57	74	62	54	36
Totals (275)	100	100	100	100	100	100

twice as often as it so identifies the Catholic college alumni (21%). Whether or not the more achievement-oriented professors chose the non-Catholic institution, or were socialized *by* it, cannot be here determined. The consistency with which the public secondary school and the non-Catholic college graduates have been the more frequently identified as publishing professors favors an interpretation emphasizing the different socialization environments. As in the Catholic secondary school, the values and role models presented to the majority of the professors in their college days did not prepare them for the independent, critical, achievement-oriented requirements of scholarly research and publication.

This view is reinforced by the generally similar distribution of the publishing and non-publishing professors as to the type of institution at which those with Ph.D's studied. Thus, while 80% of the publishing professors have Ph.D.'s (35.5% from Catholic universities and 55.2% from non-Catholic universities) less than half of the Catholic Ph.D.'s (46%) have publishing indices of 3 or 4 compared to 64% of their colleagues with doctoral degrees from non-Catholic universities. These data not only describe the special importance of doctoral study for publication performance (only 7.9% of those without doctorates are included in the publishing group) but they again identify this type of academic role as more frequently internalized in institutions other than Catholic.

The data also indicate that the non-publication status of many Catholic academicians may be related to a range of other inhibiting factors. The statistical odds favoring publication, for example, appear to be higher when the doctoral degree is initially identified as the goal of graduate study, when the student follows a full-time rather than a part-time program and completes his degree requirements as soon as possible, doing so before accepting a full-time staff appointment, and when, especially at the doctoral level, he enjoys the teaching and research advantages of a fellowship.

These advantages, as the materials of Chapter V indicated, were not too frequently found in the academic life histories of the Catholic academic men. Added to the generally non-achievement-oriented environments of their school socialization at all levels, they provide bases for explaining the non-publication status of the majority of the Catholic college professors.

Summary

The research data confirm the much-publicized impression that the Catholic college academicians have a relatively poor record of professional achievement measured in publication terms. Only 23% of the sample had distinctive records of achievement along these lines, while a majority had no publications at all, beyond theses.

Proportionate to their representation in the sample, the publishing minority were laymen more often than religious, natural scientists more often than professors in the humanities, and on the staffs of the larger rather than the smaller institutions.

Why they published while their colleagues did not depended on various factors and individual cases. As a sub-group, however, it is clear that the values and motivation needed to publish were more frequently present to their family and school socialization experiences than they were to those of their non-publishing colleagues.

The picture here is much the same as that found in the structure of faculty values. The publishing group, like the research-oriented, were the sons of parents who had the higher educational and occupational achievements and were less authoritarian. Similarly, they were more often the graduates of non-Catholic secondary schools, colleges, and universities.

The non-publishing professors, on the other hand, were socialized in families more strongly religious and less culturally advantaged, and they were also socialized in the Catholic educational system from elementary school through the university.

VIII

SCHOLARSHIP AND
THE INSTITUTIONAL SETTING

For the Catholic academic man, the familial and educational bases of his professional stature are less immediate and less meaningful than the forces that operate in his present work situation. He would not deny the influence of these pre-professional socialization factors. But he would insist that the type and quantity and quality of his scholarship are more importantly related to the structure and features of the institutional setting in which he now works.

What are the major features of the Catholic professors' work situation? What relationships, if any, do these features have with their professional perceptions and performances? And, the question of "reality" aside, how do Catholic academic men *define* their professional situations? These questions ask more than a single survey can answer because the work situations of the academicians and their definitions of them include so many and such diverse elements. In pilot form, however, the research materials identify two major sets of situational forces as especially significant. These are not unique sets of forces in academic life, but their composition and relevance in Catholic higher education are in certain respects distinctive. Broadly described, these features include (a) the physical dimensions of the work situation, and (b) the Catholic academicians' evaluations of their work environment.

THE WORK SITUATION

In general outline, the elements of the Catholic academicians' work situation are essentially the same as those present to their non-Catholic university colleagues. These include not only the administrative policies and procedures but the whole range of such professionally relevant aspects as curricula, teaching loads, class sizes, libraries, laboratories, offices, etc. On the human side they include, too, the critically important influences of administrators, colleagues, and students: but these, unfortunately, can be analyzed only indirectly and partially here. The research data focus primarily on the observable and partially measurable relationships between academic performance and the technical and physical dimensions of the institutional setting. These latter features are most conveniently described under the headings of (a) administrative policies and practices, (b) work loads, and (c) supporting services.

Policies and Practices

The heart of the matter in the Catholic professors' work situation is the religious character of administrative policies and practices. This institutional feature not only distinguishes the professional setting of the Catholic college from the majority of non-Catholic colleges but it defines the key elements of the framework within which the Catholic academic man pursues his professional career. In their specific form these elements vary somewhat by college, and they vary, too, in the extent and degree to which they affect the performance of individual professors.

But these variations do not substantially alter the structural fact that religious considerations are at the root of some of the major administrative policies and practices relevant to the Catholic academicians' work situation and professional performance.

The most important of these functionally significant religious considerations are those defining the objectives of Catholic colleges and universities and those describing their institutional structures of authority. The former prescribe not only a distinctive and many-sided institutional environment but a core curriculum in theology and philosophy tailored to the pursuit of goals and truths of mixed religious and intellectual content. The latter define the ecclesiastical status of the college and the extra-academic bias which this introduces into the policy formulation and practices of the Catholic college.

Whether or not these special sources of influence on academic policy and practice are inherently or only accidentally significant to the work situation of the Catholic professor is here irrelevant. The critical fact is that many of the faculty members interviewed perceive them as directly or indirectly inhibiting the professional structure of the situation in which they work.

Concerning the religious objectives of the Catholic college and the curriculum requirements of theology and philosophy, the members of the faculty are generally sympathetic. Not surprisingly these objectives are endorsed most strongly by the priest-professors, but the majority of the lay members of the faculty concur because their own academic backgrounds emphasized these values and identified them as the basis for the existence of a Catholic college and its unique claim to distinction.

What disturb many of the professors are the specific situational consequences that so often accompany this curricular emphasis on theology and philosophy. Some, for example, are disturbed by the policies and practices that "overemphasize" theology and philosophy and accordingly frustrate the prospects of curriculum change or of adequate concentration in each student's "major" discipline. Others are critical of the doctrinaire approach of some theologians and philosophers to their subjects and the consequences of this for the intellectual climate of the institution. Others are concerned by the professional losses incurred because of administrative wariness about recruiting non-Catholics to the staff, especially in such "delicate" areas as the behavioral sciences. Still others are bothered, but seldom seriously, by the omnipresence of religious symbols or by the frequency of religious "days off."

These familiar criticisms of administrative policies and practices have their parallels, of course, in all non-Catholic colleges. The significant fact here is that the Catholic professor specifically identifies some of the religiously-oriented policies and practices as dysfunctional features of his work situation. For the most part, these policies do not directly affect his own academic performance, but they symbolize the ambivalent posture toward scholarship often found in Catholic colleges and universities.

A more directly work-related set of consequences stems from the ecclesiastical status of the Catholic college. Each institution operates, of course, under a state charter and necessarily organizes its administrative policies and practices according to these legal requirements and to the regulations of the appropriate accrediting organizations. But the Catholic college's first charter is issued by the Church. This document places the institution under the complex and detailed law of the Church and establishes the structure of authority and procedures which control academic policies and practices. Historically these envisioned the ordained and professed religious as their primary subjects. The contemporary fact is that these ecclesiastically-oriented struc-

tures of authority and procedure now have direct consequences
for the work situations and careers of Catholic and non-Catholic
lay professors.

The facts are well known. In Catholic colleges and universities,
the ultimate authority for major academic policies and practices
resides *outside the college,* in the office of the ecclesiastically-
defined superior of the religious group chartered to administer
the institution. This authority-figure (the bishop in the case of
a diocesan college and the provincial superior in the case of a
congregation-administered college) does not usually concern
himself with every academic policy and practice but represents
a formal negative authority. The immediate deliberative authority is entrusted to the priests and brothers who, as presidents
and trustees of the institutions, are appointed by, and directly
responsible to, the extra-university ecclesiastical official. Basically
this also explains why the deans in Catholic colleges are almost
always religious and why, even at the departmental level, the
qualified priest is more likely to be chairman than his lay colleague is. Structurally, therefore, the work situation of the Catholic religious and lay professor is defined and controlled by policies
and practices on which they need not be consulted and to which
religious considerations have a pervasive relevance.

The research materials confirm the reality of this non-faculty-
defined work situation. Some professors said that they had an
informal voice in, or were consulted on, some policy matters,
but this group was a distinct minority. The majority reported a
contrary situation, in a variety of tones. Some priests and laymen
did not want "to get involved" and were content with their non-
involvement. Others, especially among the laymen, were disturbed by their professional disenfranchisement, and were not
optimistic about the prospects of change. "It's *their* college"
was a frequent description of the situation. Like the laymen in

the Church (is it *their* Church?), the majority of the lay professors in Catholic colleges felt that they were the objects of
policies and practices rather than subjects in their formulation
and implementation. They understood the "set-up" and the traditional bases on which it had developed, but in increasing
numbers their professional self-consciousness began to chafe at
the paternalistic definition of their roles. To protect and to promote the professional elements of their work situations within this
authority structure, they turned to extra-university professional
groups. Thus, during the past few years numerous Catholic college campuses have seen dormant AAUP chapters revived and
new chapters established. These units have had little attraction
for the priest-professors (because of the potential conflict-situa-
tion in which membership might place them vis-à-vis their
religious superiors), but they have symbolized the lay professors'
need for a professionally-oriented rather than a religiously-
oriented authority base for work policies and practices.

On more specific levels, it is equally clear that work-situation
policies and practices in Catholic colleges have historically envisioned a religious rather than a religious-lay faculty. In such a
structure, the fraternal voice of the faculty could be heard in the
"house" as well as in the office, and it could be listened to, or
ignored, on religious bases in the same places. Similarly, for the
priest-professors of such a college, contracts were unnecessary,
faculty manuals superfluous, promotions vainglorious, and sabbaticals a luxury. There was little need for formal concern with
these and other aspects of the work situation, because the faculty
were first and foremost priests and religious.

The post-war invasion of the lay professor found few Catholic
colleges administratively prepared for the new academic work
world. He was a new species and he lived in a different professional world. Few, if any, Catholic college presidents and deans

had ever had any first-hand experience with the *desiderata* of policies concerning contracts, promotions, tenures, sabbaticals, etc., or with the "big business" fiscal world into which the enrollment boom projected them. Their apprenticeships had been non-academic and non-business, and their new roles were not easily learned and played. And to complicate the situation further, they were selected from a regionally limited cadre of religious, to serve, as rector-presidents, for a canonically limited period of time.

These facts explain in important part the halting pace at which the work situation in Catholic colleges has been redefined according to professionally acceptable policies and practices. At present, the majority recognize the professional needs and values of these work dimensions, but they have often temporized in their adoption and vacillated in their application. Financial and personnel considerations here, as in non-Catholic colleges, have importantly conditioned this process of change, and partially explain the institutional differences which exist. The persisting and unique fact about the Catholic academicians' work situation is its involvement in a non-academic structure of religious authority and in an environment still conditioned by religious definitions of the professional setting.

Work Loads

A specific, if indirect, measure of this ambiguous source of the policies and practices defining the Catholic professor's work situation is his work load. The data of Chapter V quantitatively described this as generally heavy, both in class hours and in extra-curricular assignments. Without the added details of class sizes, number of preparations, course levels, etc., these identify only a gross situation: but the interview materials tend to confirm its definition as a heavy work load. The critical question is: what implications do these faculty work loads have for the professors' scholarly activities?

The research findings confirm, if confirmation is needed, the negative publication consequences of the heavy teaching schedule of Catholic professors. Again this is a relationship examined independent of all the other pre-professional and contemporary forces significant to publication performance. Subject to that qualification, the facts are as follows: of those teaching less than six hours, 45% have high publishing indices, compared to 36% of those who teach six to nine and ten to twelve hours and 13% of those who teach thirteen or more hours per week. Here the significant finding is not the higher publishing record of those with the lightest teaching loads, but the evidence that 36% and 13% of those with loads in excess of nine hours have still managed to publish as much as they have. It clearly suggests that the publishing performance of some Catholic professors is being achieved despite work situations which are otherwise demanding of their time and energies.

It cannot be argued, except presumptively and selectively, that these and other professors would publish more if they were less burdened by teaching assignments. At the same time the explicit, if independent, relationship between the generally low publication record of the Catholic academicians as a group and their generally heavy teaching loads forces one to conclude that publication scholarship is not fostered by their academic work situations. By inference the same consequences for teaching scholarship might be expected.

This negative picture is compounded by the evidence that the research-oriented professors are generally more involved in classroom work than their other colleagues. Only 27% of those manifesting this orientation taught less than twelve hours per week compared to over 40% of those who were ambivalent, teaching-, or dual-oriented. Moreover, not only is the proportion of the research-oriented faculty who are scheduled for twelve hours per week greater than the others; the proportion teaching thirteen or more hours is also significantly greater.

The reasons for all this are not provided by the research data. The irony is that those who are research-oriented are least likely to have time to pursue their interests, because of their heavier class schedules. This may help to explain, too, why the research-oriented professors, younger as a group than the other academic men, have not achieved more in publication terms. Some, it may safely be assumed, have their research and publication potential aborted or thwarted by their heavy teaching commitments.

Supporting Services

Observation, rather than statistical data, provides the basis for a similarly critical evaluation of other work situation features. Again, the traditional image of a clerical faculty has not been an irrelevant factor, but here, clearly, financial considerations also play an important part.

Like most other American colleges and universities, the Catholic ones have been preoccupied with the problem of expanding their physical plants in anticipation of the projected student population increase in the late 1960's. Financial commitments for classroom building, dormitories, libraries, laboratories, chapels, gymnasia, student unions, etc., are outstanding concerns on every campus and for every administrator. The substantial improvement of faculty salaries has also been a high-priority feature of this collegiate scene and an increasingly significant budget consideration, as the number of lay faculty has increased and the competition for their services has become more intense.

Few, if any, Catholic institutions have been able to achieve their goals in all areas, because their income resources have been largely limited to student tuitions, and they have not had the aid of substantial endowments. Almost every college has its "development fund campaign," but the competition for the developmental dollar is so intense, and the number of potentially big donors among Catholics is so small, that the prospects for universal success are clouded.

In this situation, and working out of an historical context which provided only an inadequate basis for faculty-centered professional development (see Chapter II), priorities have been assigned to equipment and facilities related to the instructional role of the faculty. The libraries and laboratories which have been expanded and added in this process have substantially improved the work situation of the Catholic academic man and have contributed to his professional growth and development. Only seldom, however, have these facilities and equipment been so specialized as to have unique value for his research goals. The larger universities have, of course, provided more opportunities and incentives along this line, but here, too, the historical gaps to be filled, and the rapid development of new professional equipment and facility needs, have posed expensive problems. To whatever degree possible, however, these featurs of the professional work situation are now being generally provided.

Perhaps the most conspicuous areas where equipment and facilities are in short supply are those concerned with faculty offices and with personnel aides. These problems are also present to the faculty of non-Catholic colleges, but, again, no basis for reliable comparison exists. It is simply clear from observation that the luxury of a private, or even semi-private, office or work setting is enjoyed by very few Catholic academic men. In some institutions, a lounge is their only non-classroom retreat, and neither its appointments nor its size provides much opportunity for work and privacy. Other faculty members have "desks" for offices, but these are so close to so many other "desk-offices" that conversation is the rule and academic work less likely.

Whether or not the availability of an office would materially affect the professional performance of the faculty member is an open question: the absence thereof may be only a minor handicap to those who are highly motivated by professional standards and goals. The less dedicated academician, however, in both his teaching and research activities is rendered less capable of growing intellectually and professionally.

The prevalence of this problem in Catholic colleges derives in part, of course, from their financial limitations. It also reflects the problems which Catholic institutions and their religious administrators are confronting as they perceive the "needs" of the professionally-minded lay academician, newly arrived on the scene. During the period of the religious faculty member's statistical dominance of the Catholic college staff, separate offices were less necessary and therefore not provided. The priest and the brother lived on campus. The priest-professor's home and office were joined in his room, and to its nearby sanctuary he could retreat for work and study.

By way of contrast, the lay member of the faculty is "at work" and "away from home." Except for his class and laboratory hours, he is unattached to a work situation unless office facilities are provided. The intellectual life cannot be examined properly or adequately in terms of time and motion economies, etc., but there can be little doubt that the availability of such a necessary work facility does make a difference to the quantity and quality of academic work.

Much the same situation prevails, and for much the same reasons, relative to the availability of technical services and aides.

Observation again is the basis for reporting that the Catholic college faculty member has only limited stenographic, clerical, or other professional assistance. In some universities such services are provided by graduate assistants, but this is a partial deflection from the purposes for which such assistantships were initially established.[1] Other institutions will provide these kinds of assistance on request or in special circumstances, but they are generally inadequate to the needs of the total faculty—or, at least, to the maximum facilitation of each member's goals.

The costs of such services, and the uncertainty of their optimum use even if provided, give reasons for pause. It is true, too, that they are only auxiliary to the professional work of the academic man and that the highly motivated professor will not be unduly affected by their inadequacy or absence. He may, however, find a more positively helpful work situation in another college, or, short of that, he may be less effective and less productive than his ability and the aspirations of the college can profitably tolerate.

To summarize, religiously-influenced policies and practices plus the impact of a heavy teaching load and the shortage of supporting services have bedeviled the work situation of the Catholic college faculty member. It is important to add that these problem areas have been recognized and are being steadily improved and that they are not absent, either, from many non-Catholic colleges. They are significant here because the professional stature of the Catholic academic man can only be properly evaluated when this work situation and its implications are placed in proper focus.

AS THE FACULTY SEE IT

A different but related order of evidence bearing upon the professional situation of the Catholic academic man is the structure of his attitudes toward the institutional setting of Catholic higher education. On the premise, therefore, that faculty definitions of their situation are functionally as significant as the empiric situations themselves, the religious and lay members of the research sample were asked a concluding open-ended evaluation question. Specifically, each was asked to indicate—on the basis of observation and experience—some of the major satisfactions and some of the major frustrations experienced by the faculty member of Catholic colleges.

Satisfactions

Table 20 summarizes the Catholic professors' definitions of

Table 20.—Institutional Sources of Satisfactions of Catholic
Academicians by Religious - Lay Status
(Frequency in Numbers)

Satisfaction	Religious	Laymen	Total
Catholic environment	35	75	110
Faculty cordiality	25	58	83
Academic freedom	23	44	67
Ultimate values	20	35	55
Type of student	12	36	48
Absence of pressure	5	24	29
Research facilities	3	9	12
Student-faculty closeness	3	7	10
Security	3	3	6
No satisfactions	2	9	11
No answer	22	25	47

the institutional sources of their major work satisfactions. These data, described in terms of the numerical frequency with which each satisfaction was identified, reveal some important differences not only in faculty satisfactions but in the degree to which the religious and lay professors perceive the same feature as satisfying.

As the faculty see it, the major satisfactions associated with teaching in Catholic colleges are those related not to professional but to religious and personal values. This pattern is clearly indicated in the evidence that the two most frequently identified satisfactions are the "Catholic environment" and the "cordiality" of their personal relations with their colleagues. Proportionately these identifications were made somewhat more frequently by the lay than by the clerical professors, but this difference was not very significant. It is quite likely that the "Catholic environment" was taken for granted as a major satisfaction by many religious respondents. A similar assumption, complicated by the fraternal character of the personal relations among the religious staff, may explain their lesser appreciation of the cordiality of the faculty.

An especially interesting fact is the ranking of "academic freedom" as the third most frequently identified faculty satisfaction. As this satisfaction was described in the interview, it did not refer so much to the institution's openness to the pursuit of truth, regardless of where it might lead, but to the absence of close administrative supervision of syllabi, calendars, teaching methods, etc. Academic freedom in the former sense, it should be noted, is much more present to the Catholic college than some non-Catholics, and even Catholic academicians, realize. The majority of the respondents here described probably do not think in these terms because they are generally "safe" and "orthodox" in their theological and philosophical orientations.

This view is reinforced by the fact that the fourth- and fifth-ranking satisfactions are broadly related to the concern of Catholic colleges with ultimate values, and to the type of student they attract. With few exceptions, therefore, the Catholic professors' positive perceptions focus on the religious and human dimensions of their work satisfactions. The infrequent reference to such technically professional bases of satisfaction as research facilities, etc., is in itself a significant index.

Frustrations

On the other side of the ledger, those situations defined by the Catholic academicians as institutional sources of frustration draw a more complex pattern.[2] As Table 21 indicates, the most

Table 21.—Institutional Sources of Frustrations of Catholic
Academicians by Religious - Lay Status
(Frequency in Numbers)

Frustration	Religious	Laymen	Total
Religious-lay problems	19	79	98
Salary	26	62	88
Absence of research money	16	32	48
Weak intellectual tone	20	24	44
Administration	20	20	40
Heavy teaching loads	17	10	27
Inferior students	6	10	16
Absence of pressure	6	7	13
No frustrations	3	9	12
No answer	10	15	25

clear-cut problem in terms of frequency is that involving the structure of religious-lay relationships. These frustrations, perceived most frequently by the lay professors, were described in the interviews as not involving personal relationships, but as being based on the laymen's dissatisfaction with their status in Catholic colleges. Almost 50% of the lay academicians felt that they were "second-class citizens," "necessary evils," or "without any significant voice." Approximately 20% of the religious professors sympathetically identified this as a frustration also, and some of these felt that, as far as being denied any significant voice in the affairs of the college went, they were as one with their lay colleagues.[3] Proportionately, however, the clerical professors expressed more concern about the salary situation of the lay faculty than they did about their status problems. And in a denial of the primacy of their financial self-interest, the laity defined their status dilemma as a frustration more frequently than they did their salary problems. Together these two considerations constitute about 50% of all the frustrations identified by the faculty respondents.

The professional character of these frustrations, especially that of the lay academicians' status, is repeated in the majority of the other institutional sources of faculty-defined problems. In rank order, these include the absence of research monies, the weakness of the intellectual tone of the college, the professional quality of the religious administrators, and the heavy teaching schedules. It is also interesting to find that the "absence of pressure," defined in negative terms here by thirteen professors, was a source of satisfaction to more than twice as many (29) of their colleagues. The clerical and lay professors appear, in sum, to be personally quite happy but professionally frustrated in their institutional setting.

Summary

In their present work situations, Catholic professors are inhibited in their opportunities for scholarly achievement by the structure of academic policies and practices, by their heavy work loads, and by the absence of supporting services. These conditions vary, of course, by college, and they vary, too, in their relevance for the academic performance of individual professors. Some achieve scholarly success in spite of the institutional setting in which they work; others would not grow in stature whatever the policies, load, or services.

These facts aside, the research data describe the professionally desirable aspects of an academic work situation as still only partially available to the faculty. The absence of any significant faculty voice in the formulation of policies and practices is particularly noted by the Catholic professors as a source of frustration and tension. They are disturbed, too, by the heavy teaching schedules which most of them carry, and by the absence of research facilities.

These complaints of the Catholic college faculty are not unique to them, but their situation in many of these respects is often less good than it would be in comparable non-Catholic institutions. To the import of their professional values and role perceptions these institutional settings add little. They may not inhibit the scholarship of the few, but they may abort the prospects of professional growth of the many.

As they perceive their situations, however, the greatest frustration, especially of the lay professors, is their "second-class citizen" status. They recognize the structural basis of this in the religious administration of the college, but their numerical majority and their increasing professional sensibilities have made it less and less tolerable. This does not directly affect their performance as scholars, but it has shaped an environment which "makes a difference" in their work situations. On the personal side they are generally happy and satisfied with the advantages provided them in Catholic colleges. These are not insignificant gains, but they are countered by the professional costs to scholarly achievement which co-exist with them in the institutional setting.

CATHOLIC HIGHER EDUCATION

PART FOUR

CATHOLIC HIGHER EDUCATION

IX

CONCLUSIONS

The purpose of this chapter is not to summarize the foregoing empiric materials about the academic man in the Catholic college but to generalize on their basis about the major problems and prospects of Catholic higher education in the United States. It hardly needs saying that the faculty inevitably plays a key role in any educational system. The Catholic professors do not equal the system of Catholic higher education, but the view from their angle is more comprehensive and more extensive than any other. Whatever Catholic higher education is, and whatever it may become, the clerical and lay members of the faculty are its cornerstones.

The generalizations that follow are, therefore, based in part on the survey findings, but they are not restricted by its specified foci. Some of them are still without research underpinnings; others are projections which only the future can deny or confirm. All of them center on facts and questions which are uniquely the concern of Catholic college administrators and professors. They are described under the broad headings of (1) the facts, (2) the problems, and (3) the projections.

The Facts

Almost any attempt to describe the contemporary situation in Catholic higher education will be necessarily selective and incomplete. The following facts are not, therefore, presented as an attempt to describe the situations in individual colleges or to identify the recent and continuing changes that color their accuracy and pertinence. They are based on the patterns and processes which distinguish Catholic higher education as a system. These patterns and processes are the "hard facts" that constitute the basis for critical evaluation of the problems of today and the prospects for tomorrow. There are many such "hard facts," but in concentrated form these are the most important.

Fact 1. The system of Catholic higher education in the United States is a formal involvement of the Catholic Church in the intellectual life which in spirit, size, and organization has no historic or contemporary parallel. It is a system, therefore, which is a unique venture of American Catholicism.

Fact 2. The foundation and growth of Catholic colleges and universities were not inspired by intellectual goals as ends in themselves. They were responses to the nineteenth-century mission and minority status of the Church in the United States. They were established to provide pre-seminary education for prospective priests and to protect the spiritual and moral formation of Catholics from the secular and anti-Catholic influences of other institutions. They sought to transmit religiously-approved cultural values and to integrate all new knowledge with the teachings of the Church. In sociological terms, they served primarily pattern-maintenance and integrative functions for the Church in this country.

Fact 3. The primacy of these pattern-maintenance and integrative functions and the almost exclusively clerical composition of the nineteenth-century, educated, Catholic community combined to place Catholic higher education within the structure of ecclesiastical authority. The Catholic college professor was almost always a priest, and he was assigned to teach by, and was responsible for what he taught only to, his religious superiors. In objectives and in structure the Catholic college was an extension of the teaching mission of the Church.

Fact 4. The imprint of these functions and of their ecclesiastical sponsorship has at once distinguished Catholic higher education from most other American systems and defined the structural sources of its organization, growth, and spirit. This is seen in the curriculum organization, which followed the models of the classical European secondary school and the seminary; in the proliferation of collegiate foundations throughout the nineteenth century on the orders or invitations of bishops who were in need of vocations and were fearful of secular influences; and in the subordination of the intellectual to the moral functions of collegiate education. As Fr. Ong has noted, this configuration tended to emphasize the integrity of the person at the expense of the integrity of the subject matter.

Fact 5. These religiously-derived characteristics of Catholic higher education were etched more deeply and were sharpened in detail by the coincidence of specific historical factors. Thus, the continuation into the twentieth century of the immigrant sources of Catholic population growth reinforced the felt need of the Church authorities to emphasize the pattern-maintenance functions of their colleges. Similarly, the defensive, minority-group posture of American Catholicism throughout this period sharply reduced the openness of college administrators to the dominant non-Catholic intellectual values and attitudes.

Fact 6. The domination of American Catholicism by the Irish immigrants and their descendants has been a many-sided socio-cultural source of influence on the persistence of these person-centered educational values. The Irish family was the first and most important socializing agent for the majority of American

Catholics. Its often "angelic" emphasis on narrowly perceived religious values, and its socialization of the young in diffuse and particularistic values and attitudes, helped support the pattern-maintenance functions of Catholic colleges. The products of these socialization processes in the Irish family were more often than not dependent, submissive, pietistic, and intellectually incurious.

Fact 7. These non-intellectual, non-achievement qualities were typically deepened as personality characteristics by the socialization experienced in the extensive Catholic elementary and secondary school systems. They were modeled and taught by the religious teachers of these schools. And, in only a lesser degree, they were the values, attitudes, and patterns of academic behavior to which students were exposed in the clerically-staffed pre-1950 Catholic college as well. Extensive research evidence proves that this type of socialization is uncongenial to the requirements of the intellectual life and of scholarly excellence.

Fact 8. The configuration of all these facts explains the ambiguous image so often projected by contemporary Catholic colleges and the lesser stature of the Catholic academician. The majority of the administrators and professors of Catholic colleges have had their personalities formed and their intellects developed by these systems or forces. They are what they are because of them.

Fact 9. Within the limits of these theological, structural, historical, and cultural facts, it is still a fact that American Catholic colleges and their faculties have served the goals of the Church and the nation well. Despite the special handicaps of limited resources and personnel they have broadened and deepened the knowledge and the life of the spirit; they have served as a "loyal opposition" to the excesses of secularism and scientism; they have provided at their own great sacrifice a social escalator for the mobility aspirations of thousands of the sons of immigrants; and they have graduated to the Church and the nation a host of their leaders. On the specifically academic side they have contributed most effectively as the skilled transmitters of traditional knowledge and as the logical whetstones of critical thought.

Fact 10. Since the end of World War II, Catholic higher education has been a system in transition. The GI Bill and the nation's increasing need for college-educated citizens have not been unimportant factors in this development. They helped to provide institutional stability, to promote the upgrading of the educational training of the clerical staff, and to speed the growth, to the point where they have achieved a faculty majority, of the number of lay professors—professors who are trained to, and subject to, professional standards; and, finally, they helped to increase sensitiveness to the curriculum and professional developments of other American colleges. The more significant fact, however, is that these forces coincided in time with the dynamic evolution of inner forces for change both within the universal Church and within American Catholicism. Together all these factors constitute the bases for evaluations of the contemporary problems and projections of Catholic higher education. In historical perspective they mark the "coming of age" of Catholic colleges and universities in the United States, their transition from a prolonged intellectual adolescence to a point where they can face the challenges of maturity.

The Problems

The problems of Catholic higher education as a system in transition are facts of a different order. Many of them are problems shared by other American colleges, the problems of finance and staff, of teaching and research, of conserving the gold of their intellectual heritage and of seeking its enrichment, etc. These are not new problems for either Catholic or non-Catholic colleges, but today they are seemingly more acute than ever.

On the Catholic college campus, these problems have their own special dimensions. They are imbedded in the ideological, structural, and historical contexts of the foregoing facts, which are unique in themselves. But the more significant fact is that these contexts of higher education are being challenged by persistent pressures both from within and without. Because they are so complex and so immediate, the isolation, weighting and dating of the problems they pose are especially difficult. Here they are described in terms of their primary sources outside of, or within, the system of Catholic higher education.

Since their post-war "coming of age," Catholic colleges and universities have been under increasing pressures to come to terms with the predominantly secular orientation of the American academic scene. In practical terms, they have been called upon to reduce the curriculum requirements in theology and philosophy and to desacralize the intellectual approaches to these and to other disciplines. This has seldom been the kind of adjustment on which a consensus was to be found. Often it involved a curriculum change which the lay members of the faculty and the students favored but which many of the clerical professors stoutly resisted. In many colleges administrative delays and token changes have forestalled—and still are forestalling—the kinds of change in curriculum and intellectual approach which these external—and often internal—pressures would designate. The fact is, however, that even though these changes have been uneven in scope and depth, few Catholic colleges have been able to ignore them altogether.

In part, at least, the colleges have been forced to adjust because such curricula and emphases were not well received by the intellectual, financial, and political elites who have controlled the many resources needed for institutional growth and development. The images which these elites have had of Catholic colleges have been based not infrequently on ignorance. The decisive fact is that the images have persisted in these powerful circles, and this is as much a reflection on the Catholic colleges as on their critics. In recent years, many Catholic colleges have become image-conscious and have sought not only to find out more precisely the kind of image which they did project, but the kind of image they should project, in order to increase their eligibility for hard resources and for recognition. Some of the problems of today's Catholic colleges have their roots in these external pressures and considerations.

It would be inaccurate to refer the basic problems of the Catholic college to these pressures from outside the system. Indeed, these pressures have been accepted as legitimate in some quarters only because they have been congruent to parallel forces within the Church and within the cultural sub-system of American Catholicism. These internal pressures to change are the core problems of American Catholic higher education.

Briefly stated, the "coming of age" of American Catholic colleges has been a transition ushered in, so to speak, by fundamental challenges to the validity and viability of the theological, structural, and historic warrants of the pre-1950 system. Thus, the newly developed theological formulations of the relationships between the order of faith and the order of knowledge have reopened the question of the functions of Catholic higher education. Similarly, the evolution of a theology of the laity in the Church has pressed for a re-evaluation of the status and role of the lay professor in the Catholic college. And finally, these theologically rooted pressures have become academically relevant because the lay professors constitute a faculty majority and because the American Catholic community is composed of a more highly educated, more articulate, more knowledgeable population than it was even fifty years ago. It is the combination of these internal pressures that defines the dynamic problems of the Catholic college. They are the problems of the "coming of age" of Catholic higher education in the United States.

Problem 1. What is the meaning of the adjective "Catholic" as a qualifier of the noun "higher education"? Essentially this is the core problem, as far as identifying the objectives of Catholic colleges and universities goes. It presses for re-examination now because the pattern-maintenance and integrative (in the direction of socialization) functions of the intellectual and historical adolescence of the church in the United States have lost their theological and cultural bases.

The theological acceptance of the integrity of the secular-as-secular has removed the need to integrate all knowledge to a transcendental order of truth and has freed the scholar from the inhibitions and fears of self-imposed censorship and doctrinal error. Much recent theological work is its own best example of the intellectual openness which these premises prescribe. It does not remove the continuing importance of the pattern-maintenance functions of Catholic colleges for the Church, nor does it abdicate the responsibility of seeking to integrate the orders of supernatural and natural truth. At the college and university levels, however, these commitments are seen as secondary to the intellectual work at hand, the scholarly work of discovering and transmitting the validated knowledge of each order of reality according to its own terms.

This is primarily an adaptive function because it recognizes the evolutionary character of man's pursuit of truth and the consequent need for an open and flexible system. Its primacy as the function of tomorrow's Catholic college derives from these inner sources. On the cultural side, it is reinforced by the fact that the American Catholic community has recently achieved a social acceptance and an intellectual level which no longer will tolerate education in pattern-maintenance terms. Much of the self-criticism of Catholics is proof of this, whatever the initial inspiration of this self-criticism. The mid-twentieth-century American Catholic has spiritual and intellectual challenges to meet which a non-adaptation-oriented system of higher education cannot satisfy.

This formulation of the fundamental problem of Catholic colleges presupposes a number of propositions which are not empirically self-evident. It assumes, for example, that a de-nominational college and its faculty can make an intellectual commitment and can freely follow this commitment wherever it leads them. It assumes, therefore, that the adjective "Catholic" can precede the noun "higher education" without any necessary loss to the attributes of either. The facts are that this has seldom been realized. The nineteenth-century definition of the Catholic college is still a powerful force in administrative councils and in faculty role-perceptions. The transition to a new conception of academic functions and roles is still to be fully realized. The problem of the objectives of Catholic higher education in the twentieth century is still unresolved. A direction has been pointed, but it is still to be followed.

Problem 2. How can the Catholic college realize its intellectual goals, and at the same time function within the separate and different structures of religious and professional authority? This problem of organizational structure and authority is unique in Catholic colleges primarily in relation to the extra-academic power of religious superiors. Its analogue in public institutions is the extra-academic power of political bodies.[1] On the Catholic campus, however, it is a problem newly arrived because, until the lay professors achieved their present overall majority, the formal significance of professional concerns was minimal.

Prior to this period the college administration and the faculty were priests or brothers, and these roles defined their first and most powerful loyalties. They were not independent professional persons but subordinate officers in a bureaucratic organization. Obedience to the authority of religious superiors was a primary expectation and this, not because of their technical claims to competence and authority, but because they were the ecclesiastically appointed religious superiors. In the practical order, the exercise of this religious authority by superiors, and its interpretation by the clerical professors as something properly requiring obedience, varied by individuals. The dominant authority values, however, were clearly those of the bureaucratic rather than the professional structure.

The advent of the lay professor and the new emphasis on the adaptive functions of Catholic higher education have, therefore, posed an apparent dilemma. Can the professor in the Catholic college function as a free professional within a structure of religious authority? Ideally, of course, the answer is that he can, provided only that his teaching does not threaten the official dogmas of the Church or invade the areas of faith and morals. This literal qualification is essentially no different from that restricting the professor in the publicly supported institution from advocating anarchy or sexual promiscuity. The outer boundaries of academic freedom in both these cases are dimly drawn and are subject to various definitions.

In the case of the Catholic college, as in state colleges, the threats to academic freedom are posed most frequently by extra-academic officials who are often intellectually and professionally naive or ignorant. Such instances have been relatively few in Catholic higher education, not because the border-line issues, and uninformed officials to interpret them, were not present, but because the faculty was "safe" theologically and philosophically. Even so, the air of caution has been characteristic of Catholic college administrators, and their priestly concerns have not infrequently been aroused by the "different," "unorthodox" or "relativistic" intellectual positions of some of their professors, religious as well as lay. The prospects that such "different" positions will increase in number and in significance, as Catholic colleges and professors confront the crises of transition, recommends a careful re-study of the boundary lines defining the structures of religious and professional authority. If new goals are to be established, new structural frameworks must be designed for their realization.

Problem 3. What is to be the status of lay professors? This problem is phrased in terms of the future, because the contemporary situation of Catholic lay academicians has already been described. In spite of some recent increases in the number and types of professional opportunities provided for their responsible participation in the affairs of the college, they still clearly play a subordinate role. Their frustrations can only be expected to grow in this respect as their numbers increase and as their professional sensibilities become stronger. The problem of morale is only one dimension of the situation. Faculty dissatisfaction with their role definition is bound to entail resignations, and to affect not only the scholarly performance of the faculty but the recruitment campaign of the college.

Perhaps the most significant aspect of this problem is not so much its professional as its religious implications. Here, encapsulated in the dilemma of the lay professors' status, is the more basic problem of the role of the layman in the Church. Indeed, it is a test case par excellence. There are few, if any, agencies of lay participation in the Church in which the issue is so clearly drawn.

In the Catholic college the religious and lay members of the faculty have the same functions and the same roles and share a commitment to the goals of Catholic higher education. If the lay professor's role cannot here emerge from its "second-class citizen" status, it is difficult to think of any Church-related organization in which he could realize full citizenship. The resolution of this problem of the Catholic academy, therefore, may have repercussions outside academic halls. It may prevision the kind of role which the laity may yet achieve in the structure of American Catholicism.[2]

This problem of the lay professor's status should not obscure the fact that any significant change in it will have consequences for the role of the clerical professors. Indeed, some of them already feel that administrative preoccupation with the lay professors has penalized the scholarly potential of the clerical staff. They do not deny the layman's claim to full citizenship, but they resent the fact that as religious they are taken for granted or that their professional aspirations are deemed less deserving than those of the laity. At the moment, this is only a straw in the wind, but it may foreshadow a type of new minority protest which could follow any upgrading of the status of the lay professor. And these are only some of the more obvious complications of the problem of the lay professor's status.

Problem 4. How can the Catholic system of higher education maximize its opportunities for realizing these mid-twentieth-century goals within the structure of the Church? The tentacles of this problem extend far and wide. Here the first question is one of resources: how many Catholic colleges can American Catholics afford and staff? This problem is again not readily answerable. There are regional needs and educational goals which properly justify the foundation and the support of many institutions, small, medium, and large. Basically it is an economic problem, a problem of the allocation of resources in terms of

goals. When these goals were primarily of the pattern-maintenance and integration variety, limited resources were adequate
and available. Even so, the record of collegiate failures in Catholic higher education suggests that over-extension of the system
inevitably results in intellectual and financial waste. The supply
of qualified clerical and lay professors, let alone the money, is
simply not adequate to the demand.

This is a system problem, but it is one which has been denied
recognition because the focus has been on regional and con-
gregational, rather than on national and Church, concerns. Do the
Jesuits, for example, really have the resources in available
clerical and lay professors to staff adequately their multiple
high schools, colleges, and universities? And does the Catholic
college for women, as another example, have an adequate intellectual justification for its multiple establishments, given the
limits of staff and finances? Similarly, why are there no effective
mergers of Catholic men's and women's colleges to effect economies and to capitalize on superior staff members—especially
when only a footpath or a road physically separates two colleges?
These are some of the problems of wasted resources which
Catholic higher education can not afford to tolerate. The self-
interest of congregations and of regions, and the technical
problems of at least partial consolidation, are excuses which the
goals of Catholic higher education can no longer endure. They
are organizational and resource problems which must be re-
solved if the transition of Catholic colleges to a mature academic
status is to be achieved.

The Projections

This section of conclusions will be brief because predictability
is still an aspiration rather than a credential of the social sciences.
This fact notwithstanding, the historical and sociological per-

spectives provided by the foregoing data on Catholic higher education will serve as a basis for some selective projections. The premises on which they are based cannot be explicitly identified in every instance, but wherever possible their general character is briefly specified.

Projection 1. The rapid professional maturation of Catholic colleges and universities during the past 15 years will slow down perceptibly in the years immediately ahead. This projection is based not only on considerations of the pre-World War II base point and the "room for growth" then present, but on the limits to growth imposed by present commitments and the scarcity of resources. Thus, it is pertinent to recall that 70% of the professors interviewed were under 50 years of age and may be expected to remain on the staffs of Catholic colleges for at least another 15 years. There is, moreover, no reason to expect that many—the younger Ph.D.'s aside—will grow much in professional stature. In addition, the recruitment problems may be expected to become more difficult in a tight market increasingly favorable to sellers. Even the young Catholic Ph.D.'s now emphasize professional over religious and particularistic values and seem to be accepting non-Catholic rather than Catholic college appointments. Consequently the slow rate of performance growth which may be projected for the present faculty and the difficult problems of recruitment are personnel bases for predicting only a gradual development of the intellectual maturity of the Catholic college in the near future.

Projection 2. The primacy of the theological and philosophical concerns of the Catholic college is another portent of a relatively slow rate of change. Values of this order are most resistant to change in every social system. In the Catholic Church they are protected by a centuries-old tradition and by a complicated bureaucratic apparatus. These function to inhibit change throughout the whole Church, but they are especially significant for American Catholicism. Still in a kind of colonial status, it has experienced neither the luxury of an intellectual elite nor the crises of wholesale defections. Consequently its theologians and philosophers have seldom been speculative pioneers. They have been content to interpret the "mind of the Church" in terms of the practical problems posed on the pluralistic American scene. The administrative and vocational orientations of the hierarchy have encouraged this direction of theological thought,[3] as have the non-university climate of the seminaries in which the leading theologians and philosophers taught.[4]

During the past decade, some of the younger professors of the sacred sciences have been attracted to the more speculative and dynamic analyses of European theologians and philosophers. In some Catholic colleges these influences have been intellectually liberating, but they are still far from being dominant forces in the academic life of the institutions. In time these younger men may be expected to occupy more powerful positions and may be able to infuse the Catholic college with a more positive intellectual spirit. How long before this may come about, and how much they may be able to do, are unanswerable questions. At the moment the Catholic college administrators are like fretful mothers. Now that their institutions have come of age, they are worried about whirlwind courtships. The chances are that the marriages of most Catholic colleges to the new theological and philosophical developments will come about only after a long and worrisome engagement.

Projection 3. The status of the lay professor will gradually improve. Initially the pattern of consultative authority will be broadened to provide for faculty voting on many academic policies and practices. This will be followed by the appointment of qualified lay professors to administrative posts usually held by religious. These processes will not develop at the same time in all colleges but will vary with the size of the institution, its academic aspirations, the number and quality of the religious and lay members of the staff, and their professional aggressiveness. Much depends not only on the degree of clerical resistance to the assumption of lay leadership but on the readiness of laymen to accept the responsibilities of leadership. Short of a crisis in the supply of vocations, it is not likely that many laymen will be appointed to the office of college president and some, of course, would not accept it in any event. Some such appointments will probably accompany the increase in the number of small colleges. These and other related changes in the direction of a fuller partnership for the lay professors will be indices of maturity which may help in dramatic fashion to change the unfavorable image of Catholic colleges in some quarters.

Basically, however, it will not be merely the presence of laymen in administrative posts that will make a difference. The quality of their administrative performances and the quality of the faculty's voice in policy formulation must match the demands of the new adaptive functions of the Catholic college and university. The test of these qualitative considerations will probably be slow in coming. The speed with which they do develop and the form that they take will be interesting and significant predictors of the future role of the laymen in the Church.

Projection 4. The lessons of the past will be forgotten and, in response to the explosion of college enrollments, more Catholic colleges will be established. Some will be coeducational from the beginning and some of the existing institutions will become coeducational. Together they will still further outstrip the financial and personnel resources necessary for excellence.

This projection is based on the steady announcements of new college foundations and on the unlikelihood of any effective collaboration among separate institutions even in the same geographic area. Centuries-old differences among religious congregations will not, it appears, be readily set aside in the interests of quality education for all. And every young religious congregation will probably continue to feel the need to establish its own college as a symbol of its worth. One would like to be sanguine about such developments, but the story of the nineteenth-century Catholic college experience and the facts of the academic market place today are not hopeful auguries.

APPENDIX
FACULTY PROFILES

The following word sketches of six Catholic college professors are based upon a selective use of the interview data and on impressionistic notes written "on the scene" as time permitted. These sketches do not describe individual professors but composite representatives of three major academic types, viz., the professional scholar, the incomplete academician, and the uncommitted teacher. Each of these types, it is recognized, includes professors with characteristics quite different from those described here. Within these limitations, however, the faculty profiles are designed to add some "flesh and blood" to the foregoing statistical skeletons.

THE PROFESSIONAL SCHOLARS

Rev. Bartholomew Anderson

Father "Bart" Anderson is a hard-nosed physicist. The author of over a dozen articles in *professional* journals (his emphasis) and the chairman of a small but growing department, he was interested in the objectives of the faculty survey but frankly suspicious of its sociological auspices. He dramatized this concern by repeating almost every question. Then you could almost hear his cerebral gears click into orderly action to provide answers that were direct, pointed, and brief. The lab was waiting for him and he wanted to get back to *his own* work.

This priest-scholar was born and brought up in a middle-sized Eastern city, the eldest son of an Irish mother and a non-Catholic Scandinavian father. His mother had the stronger personality, but he talked more enthusiastically about the industry and the steadiness of his craftsman father. Except for mathematics, his academic record in Catholic grammar school, high school and college was only slightly better than average. "Math and science were fun, but I just wasn't interested in the other subjects; and from high school on I knew that I was going to be a priest." He wanted to enter the seminary on graduation from high school. But his father insisted ("Thank God, he did insist") that he first earn his Bachelor's degree in science from the college in which he is now teaching.

As Father Anderson now describes it, the seminary deepened his spiritual life and made him a priest, but "it was almost an intellectual wasteland." He admired the few professors who made him work, but he felt that "too much time was spent looking up Greek words . . . and much of the philosophy, and even the theology, wasn't related to present-day knowledge and problems." He still managed to do some scientific reading and studying, however, and after ordination was promptly sent to a Catholic graduate school for his Master's degree in physics. Only moderately satisfied with the program there, he *chose* a non-Catholic institution for his Ph.D. and was awarded it some three years later. This, unquestionably, was the big experience of his intellectual life. A deliberate and unemotional respondent to questions in other areas, he was almost lyrical as he described the intellectual ideals and standards and the love for scholarship which he found there. "It was a workout," he said, "but it was exciting because you knew you were learning and because you were so close to the new discoveries."

Almost forty years old when he received his Ph.D., Father Anderson has been in an intellectual hurry ever since. He got some early publication mileage out of his dissertation and some allied research problems, but then, as he put it, "I became involved in the busy work of university committees." The headaches and the frustrations of these years still live with him. Now these causes can enlist his moral support, but he saves his time and his energies for his own work. Science is at the center of his life.

A crusty character, Father Anderson is impatient with administrators and their red tape, and with religious superiors who are ignorant of the demands of scholarship. "I told them," he said, "that if they wanted to get a return on their investment in me, then they'd have to keep me out of parish work, retreats, and all that." He is also critical of the religious professors who "coast" and of the lay professors who see themselves in a job rather than in professional terms. "Some of the priests don't read any more," he observed, "and some of the laymen seem to think that teaching here, and only here, is their guarantee of salvation."

A hard-working, "no nonsense" teacher and researcher, Father Anderson will probably never make a *major* contribution to his discipline. Intellectually he is impressive more in his ideals and in his approach than in the breadth and depth of his knowledge. He is not the least bit concerned with the "plight of the humanities" nor with the claims of the social sciences. He is a scientist, a professional academician, respected by his colleagues and by the physics majors whose careers have been helped along by his training and recommendations. He is a priest first, of course, but his priesthood is served by his science. He is probably in the lab right now.

Dr. Arthur Buckley

This young associate professor of English is bright, articulate, industrious, and well-trained. What's more, he knows it. But at the same time he is rather insecure. He is a scholar of promise, but the question of its full realization is still open.

The intellectual promise to which his publications (one book and ten articles) are testimonials was previsioned by his happy choice of college-educated parents. Like his two brothers and two sisters, Arthur was "expected to be college material." He attended a local parish school and then commuted to the prestige high school conducted by the Jesuits. During these latter years he "thought about the priesthood," but the idea never captured his enthusiasm. He was too interested in too many other things. He was a star debater, a sodalist, a literary "buff," an honor student . . . and none of it involved much pain or strain.

In the Jesuit college which he attended the story was much the same until his Junior year. Then the scholarship and the personal interest of a lay professor in English so impressed him that he grew up in a hurry. "I began to read and think as I had never read and thought before. Instead of just going to school, I learned to work and I worked to learn." There was no question now about his career. He was going to get his Ph.D. at a major non-Catholic college and he was going to live the intellectual life.

He did just this. On the strength of his performance and strong faculty recommendations, his graduate education was marked by successive scholarships, fellowships, and assistantships. More importantly, he became the protégé of an internationally known scholar, from whom he caught the spirit of research and publication scholarship. Five hard and happy years later he had his Ph.D. and was ready to teach.

Just why he accepted an appointment at a Catholic college—he had offers from some non-Catholic institutions—he now finds hard to explain. The best that he can offer is, "I thought I would feel more comfortable there." There are times now when he second-guesses this decision and when he dreams of being invited to the staff of a large non-Catholic institution. He says that he does not want to be known as a "Catholic scholar," but he enjoys the local deference and respect that this brings him. Right now he's one of the bigger fish in a little pond and he knows it.

Concerning his own career and Catholic higher education, Dr. Buckley is ambivalent. There are days when he is encouraged by the improved intellectual caliber of his colleagues and students. There are other days when he is a leading critic of the heavy teaching loads, the absence of research support, the slowness of curriculum change, etc. He knows that because he has published he is not faring too badly by local standards. Still he works at keeping up his contacts with non-Catholic scholars, and his name-dropping now and then suggests that he is proud of their acceptance of him. He still has the unsettling feeling, however, that he is outside the mainstream of American intellectual life and that his potential is being squandered. Lately he has become even more anticlerical than he realizes. It is a type of intellectual anticlericalism rather than a personal hostility and it does not affect his faith—but it adds to his confusion.

There is no doubt that Dr. Buckley is a genuinely professional scholar. He will probably remain in Catholic higher education and, if he can overcome the problems of his work situation and his own ambivalence, he will probably continue to work hard and to publish some significant studies. He is worried about this, although consoled somewhat by the feeling that he is making a contribution to the Church. But his children go to public schools.

THE INCOMPLETE ACADEMICIANS

Rev. Daniel Catalano

Father Daniel Catalano is a Catholic priest and a Catholic philosopher, precisely in that order. He wanted to be an historian, but—that's the story of his academic life.

His story began in the strongly religious Italian family in which he grew up. His parents were born in this country and high-school educated, but they were very much a part of the Italian community. His mother was a "really holy" woman, and she brought all her children up to love God and his Church. His father, a barber by trade, had been more casual about his religion, but with two daughters in the convent and Father Dan a priest, he has become a proud and practicing Catholic.

As far back as he can recall, Father Catalano wanted to be a priest. The nuns in grammar school and the brothers in high school seemed to know this, and they encouraged both his spiritual and his academic development. He was a better-than-average student, except in mathematics and science, but he had to work for his grades. A mild and quiet boy, he was never a problem to anyone, and was an altar boy from the fourth grade on.

In part because his parents were unable to finance college for him and in part because he wanted to, Father Dan entered the minor seminary after high school. There and in the major seminary his vocation was tested and proved. There was never any real question or difficulty. He loved the spiritual and fraternal atmosphere and did not mind, as others did, the sometimes harassing details of the "rule." On the intellectual side, however, these years seem to have been less inspiring. "Some of my professors were good, some not-so-good, but I learned something from all of them." Frequently he thought of spending his priestly life in some mission field, but especially as ordination neared the prospect of being a history professor became equally attractive. In fact, he mentioned this latter interest to his superiors with the hope that he would be sent on for graduate study. "But that was the period when they sent only a few on for degrees," he explained, "and I wasn't one of them."

As a philosophy professor, Father Catalano is not, however, degreeless. He "picked up" an M.A. in philosophy through an affiliation which the seminary had with a Catholic university. He's too intellectually honest a person to define this as a professional degree, but he has worked steadily and hard to fill in the gaps and to deepen his knowledge. He reads widely and well; he quietly attends some philosophical symposia and conventions; and he has restudied the writings of the great philosophers. The trouble—and he knows it—is that these are almost exclusively Catholic philosophical resources and studies.

The one-sided incompleteness of Father Dan's philosophical training and perspective is offset in part by his priestly dedication to teaching. He has gained campus-wide recognition because his classroom standards are high, both for himself and for his students. He is bothered by the knowledge that some of his philosophical colleagues have stopped reading and stimulate (or react to) student apathy with apathy of their own. For his part, he is ready and willing to work with anyone sincerely interested in the students and in the college and insists, "I'm not opposed to change."

So far he has written only a few book reviews, and these for the congregation's own publication. He has some notes that some day he would like to write up for an article or maybe a book. But then again, he probably won't. Being a priest is a full-time job, and he enjoys the occasional work in the parish, the preaching, the counselling, etc. Besides, he wanted to be a historian, but here he is, a Catholic philosopher.

Dr. Charles Doherty

Dr. Charles Doherty is an economist with a problem. As he describes it, "It isn't really a problem, but when you have so many good things going for you, it's kind of hard to zero in on any one of them." Dr. Doherty, you see, is a good family man, an active lay Catholic, a competent teacher, and an "operator."

In a sense, his story is a Catholic version of the Horatio Alger epic. The hero was brought up in a working-class family by parents who were often overwhelmed by the problems of feeding and clothing seven children on the uncertain income of a long-shoreman. His early education was a hit-and-miss affair, conspicuous by its lack of academic promise. "The Police Athletic League saved me from a peck of trouble and I did so poorly in high school that all I hoped for was a civil service job."

The Army and the G.I. Bill, however, provided him with the motivation and the help he needed for a college education. Because he knew some friends at the local Catholic college, he enrolled there and literally worked his way through for four years. Somewhat to his own surprise he discovered that he wasn't stupid and that when he applied himself he could make out better than most. This was particularly true in Accounting and Economics. . . . "I was never one for learning for its own sake" . . . so, under a full head of steam, he decided to get a Ph.D. His M.A. work at a non-Catholic graduate school was apparently undistinguished, but he reported some relief when he found that there weren't any Communists or Socialists there. In any event, scholarships brought him back to a Catholic institution for his doctoral program and gave him his first taste of teaching. He enjoyed this, and he was challenged, too, by the problems of applying Catholic social principles to the business affairs of the day. Economic theory annoyed and depressed him.

Over the next few years, Dr. Doherty moved around among a number of different Catholic colleges. Some were stepping stones, others didn't appreciate his practical orientation, still others didn't provide him with "outside opportunities." Frequently he was tempted to leave education and to capitalize on his knowledge and skills in business, but he could never quite make the break. For that he is thankful now, because he has found his niche. An associate professor with one foot in the Economics Department and the other foot in the School of Commerce, he has worked hard at making contacts and winning recognition in both the university and the business community. As he himself admits, he has had quite a bit of success. His few "nonacademic" articles in Catholic periodicals and his ready diagnosis of economic trends in the local press have been rewarded in both worlds. He is a trusted advisor of the Dean of the School of Commerce, a valued public relations figure for the university, and a paid consultant for some local industries. On the strictly academic side he still gets to the conventions, but he has all but given up trying to keep abreast of the professional literature. He knows that he is running thin intellectually and that he has too many irons in a dying fire, but he can't seem to shake himself loose from any of his activities. A gregarious person and a facile speaker, he is a "regular" on the Holy Name banquet circuit and he can't turn down the fees offered for consultations. He is frankly proud of the attention and the deference that he gets, and he is proud, too, of the comfortable life he can provide for his family. He is ambitious, industrious, capable, and he fills a need, but he is not a scholar.

THE UNCOMMITTED TEACHERS

Rev. Francis Early

Father Francis Early always dreamed of being a parish priest or of converting the natives in some distant mission land. He did not like to read and was never a very good student. Now he is a professor.

The way this all came about is a mixture of comedy and tragedy. Fr. Early's childhood years were not very happy. His father died when he was only ten years old and his mother, a highly emotional and religious woman, smothered him with affection. She worried about his interest in sports, and worried too about his adolescent mania for scientific experiments. In the Catholic schools which he attended he was only an average student and the same was true of his work-interrupted college career. There were times when the financial problems at home and his mother's poor health discouraged him, but somehow his dream of becoming a priest persisted. He was twenty-four when he finally entered the seminary.

Father Early's seminary years were happy, if uneventful. The discipline at times annoyed him and he had his difficulties with Latin—"I still have some problems with the Breviary"—but he enjoyed the friendliness and the spiritual tone that dominated the place. He is frank to say that he wasn't a good student and that he "sweated out" his final oral examinations; but he made it. He was older than the rest of his ordination class and his record was undistinguished; but he was a priest.

The checkered pattern of his priestly career suggests that his superior sometimes had problems knowing what to do with him. He never did make the missions, but he seems to have been everywhere else and to have done everything else. He taught high school, worked in parishes, preached on a local mission band, and served as a non-teaching administrator at a college. He even served for a time as a chaplain in the Army, and this experience he *really* enjoyed. It was too good to last. For the past six years he has been an associate professor of theology.

The simple fact is that he is not a theologian and he is the first to admit it. He teaches the subject with some skill and enthusiasm, but he has neither the academic background nor the intellectual ability to go beyond the formalities of the text. "I'm an indoctrinator, and I may as well admit it," he says, "but that's all these college kids need." For all practical purposes he himself has stopped reading, but he is pleased that the younger priests are more professionally trained and more capable.

There is no doubt, however, that Father Early fills a real campus need. He is popular with the students and alumni and he is always on call for "small talk" or for advice on their problems. And he has probably officiated at more weddings of alumni than any other priest on campus. Of course, the athletes and the athletic-minded are more at home with him than are the Dean's List students because he's still "crazy about sports," but he is a friend to all.

It is not easy to capture his personality. He is a "regular guy" type of priest and a good priest, too. He touches the hearts of many of his students, but there are few traces of his influence on their minds.

Prof. Edward Flatley

Prof. Edward Flatley is a college language teacher, and there's nobody more surprised than he is. The irony is that he is frustrated by the fact of his own relative success. He didn't plan it and now he has nowhere to go.

His life story is a patchwork quilt of career stops and starts that makes his frustration understandable. A quiet, non-athletic boy, he was brought up by working-class parents who "knew where he was and what he was doing every minute." In the parochial schools which he attended, he was an average student with no real academic interests. He was attracted, however, to the priesthood, and at the end of high school he entered the diocesan minor seminary. Within two years he knew that this life was not for him, so he promptly withdrew and registered at the nearby Catholic college. There he displayed a flair for languages but nothing else. On graduation day he still didn't know what he wanted to do.

His first job, as a department store trainee, pointed him to a possible career in merchandising or in retail management, but he hated every minute of it. Fortunately, a life-line was thrown him when the French teacher in a nearby Catholic prep school died and he was offered the job. Partly to escape the store, he accepted it, and he managed to get through the year. Money was not a prime consideration because he was still single and, in any event, he enjoyed the hours and the company of the religious teachers. He stayed on and even earned his Master's degree.

Three years later, thanks to the veteran's invasion of colleges, he was offered an instructor's position in the Modern Language Department at Alma Mater. He proudly accepted it and has been there now for almost fifteen years, teaching the same basic courses on the same twelve-to-fourteen-hour schedule. In 1950 he was made an assistant professor; but, since he is without a Ph.D., that promotion seems to have marked the peak of his academic career. He did take a few "extra" courses, but with a wife and children to support now, there was not the time, the money, or the motivation to finish degree requirements.

In his present situation Prof. Flatley is an unhappy and frustrated man. He is worried about his non-tenure status. He is suspicious of the consequences, *for him,* of every new appointment and curriculum change. He avoids "shop talk" with his younger Ph.D. colleagues. He is very bitter about the administration because "they changed the requirements since I came." Professionally and economically, he is frozen in his present status.

It is a tragic situation for all concerned. The administration is, at least morally, stuck with him. For his part, there's no place else to go. As for his students, they have a high school teacher who works, frustrated and insecure, at a "job."

NOTES

1. For surveys and bibliographies of sociological research in the field of education, see: Neal Gross, "Sociology of Education" in Robert K. Merton and others, *Sociology Today* (New York: Basic Books, 1960); Orville G. Brim, *Sociology and the Field of Education* (New York: Social Science Research Council, 1958); "The Sociology of Education: A Trend Report and Bibliography," *Current Sociology,* Vol. VIII, No. 3 (1958).

2. Thorstein Veblen, *The Higher Learning in America* (New York: B. W. Huebsch, 1918).

3. Logan Wilson, *The Academic Man* (New York: Oxford, 1942).

4. Theodore Caplow and Reece J. McGee, *The Academic Marketplace* (New York: Basic Books, 1958), p. 3.

5. Recent sociological cases in point include: Rose Goldsen and others, *What College Students Think* (Princeton: Van Nostrand, 1960); James A. Davis and Norman Bradburn, *Great Aspirations: Career Plans of America's June 1961 College Graduates,* Report No. 82, National Opinion Research Center, University of Chicago (1961).

6. R. H. Knapp and H. B. Goodrich, *Origins of American Scientists* (Chicago: University of Chicago Press, 1953); R. H. Knapp and J. J. Greenbaum, *The Younger American Scholar: His Collegiate Origins* (Chicago: University of Chicago Press, 1953).

7. Caplow and McGee, *op. cit.*

8. Paul F. Lazarsfeld and Wagner Thielens, Jr., *The Academic Mind* (Glencoe: The Free Press, 1958).

9. In addition to the much-quoted findings of Knapp and Greenbaum and Knapp and Goodrich, *supra,* cf. investigations of Catholic representation in standard directories of national leaders as footnoted in John Tracy Ellis, *American Catholics and the Intellectual Life* (Chicago: The Heritage Foundation, 1956), pp. 29-30.

10. *Ibid.*

11. Thomas F. O'Dea, *The American Catholic Dilemma: An Inquiry into the Intellectual Life* (New York: Sheed and Ward, 1958).

12. *Ibid.,* pp. 155-161.

13. Justus G. Lawler, *The Catholic Dimension in Higher Education* (Westminster: Newman, 1959).

14. Catholic periodicals such as *The Commonweal, America, The Catholic World,* etc., have published a number of shorter articles on this topic in recent years. Cf. also the excerpts regarding the history and present

status of Catholic education in *American Catholicism and the Intellectual Ideal,* ed. Frank L. Christ and Gerard E. Sherry (New York: Appleton-Century-Crofts, 1961).

15. Quoted in O'Dea, *op. cit.,* p. 22.

16. Some pre-study consultants suggested that the research should be restricted to the lay professors. This view was rejected not only because the religious members of the Catholic college faculties are a significant proportion of the staff but because they also dominate the public image of Catholic higher education.

17. Statistics based on data provided in *The Official Directory of Catholic Colleges and Universities,* 1959.

18. The CCICA register has listed a large number of these Catholic educators, but their inclusion was prohibited by practical research considerations as well as uncertainty about the definitiveness of the listing.

19. A cursory check of the faculties of these professional schools indicates that many are non-Catholic and would not be included in the present study.

20. The research design provided for (1) the tabular classification of American Catholic coeducational and men's colleges by region (East, Midwest, South, West), by student enrollment (large, over 2500; medium, 1,000-2,500; small, under 1,000), and by the proportion of religious and lay professors; (2) the selection by random procedures of a sample of 22 colleges representative of the universe; (3) the random selection of 300 professors in the proportions required to provide representation by region, institutional size, and the religious-lay professor ratio. Each professor was interviewed by the author in order to guarantee uniformity of procedure and to reduce the possibility of multiple-interviewer bias.

21. Copies of the questionnaire and interview schedules are available on request to author.

CHAPTER 2

1. The best general study is that of Edward J. Power, *A History of Catholic Higher Education in the United States* (Milwaukee: Bruce Pub., 1958).

2. The standard historical studies of American higher education seldom include references to the evolution of Catholic colleges and universities.

3. Among such useful but incomplete studies are the following dissertations published by the Catholic University of America Press: Francis P. Cassidy, *Catholic College Foundations and Development in the United States, 1677-1850* (1924); Sebastian A. Erbacher, *Catholic Higher Education for Men in the United States, 1850-1866* (1931); Sr. Mary M. Bowler, *A History of Catholic Colleges for Women in the United States of America* (1933).

4. Power, *op. cit.*, p. vii.
5. *Ibid.*, p. 34.
6. *Ibid.*, pp. 54-87.
7. *Ibid.*, pp. 255-332.
8. Quoted in Richard Hofstadter and Walter P. Metzger, *The Development of Academic Freedom in the United States* (New York: Columbia University Press, 1955), p. 211.
9. *Ibid.*, pp. 211-212.
10. Cf. Sr. Mary M. Bowler, *op. cit.*
11. Across the country separate Catholic colleges for men and women are to be found not only in the same city but on adjacent properties. Proximity, however, breeds mainly student social relationships since, in almost every case, each college uneconomically maintains its separate administrative staff, faculty, library, laboratories, etc.
12. Power, *op cit.*, p. 90.
13. *Ibid.*, p. 92.
14. Many Catholics and most non-Catholics do not know that the Catholic Church in the United States was classified as a "mission" and was under the ecclesiastical administration of the Congregation for the Propagation of the Faith until 1908.
15. Power, *op. cit.*, p. 92.
16. Erbacher, *op. cit.*, p. 79.
17. Quoted by Power, *op. cit.*, p. 95, from *Report of the United States Commissioner of Education, 1872.*
18. Hofstadter and Metzger, *op. cit.*, pp. 369-383.
19. *Catholic Colleges and Schools in the United States*, Part 2 (Washington: National Catholic Welfare Conference, 1936), p. 10.
20. Cf. *The Official Directory of Catholic Colleges and Universities, 1962.*
21. The image of a religiously dominated faculty is still so commonplace that almost every lay professor receives some "Dear Father" mail.
22. W. Ong, *American Catholic Crossroads* (New York: Macmillan, 1959), p. 93.
23. Cf. "Tradition" in *The Catholic Encyclopedia* (New York: The Encyclopedia Press, 1912), Vol. XV, pp. 6-13.
24. The development of a theology of the laity has only recently become a major Church issue. Cf. Yves M. J. Congar, O.P., *Lay People in the Church*, trans. by Donald Attwater (Westminster: Newman, 1957) and the Commission on the Laity of the Second Vatican Council.
25. New Haven: Yale University Press, 1950.
26. The religious orders and congregations responsible for the administration of the majority of these Catholic colleges have usually divided their national organization into regional or province sub-groups based upon convenience and numbers. Each provincial structure is semiautonomous, and the leaders of its various organizations (parishes, hospitals, colleges, etc.) are selected from the province members.

27. Deans and department chairmen are not involved in any ecclesiastical legislation. Typically, however, the appointment of a religious to such an office is formally made by the provincial superior.

28. The matter of the Index is on the agenda of the Second Vatican Council.

29. For a discussion of the concept of the total status of the priest, see John D. Donovan, *The Catholic Priest; A Study in the Sociology of the Professions,* unpublished Ph.D. dissertation, Harvard University, 1951.

30. David Riesman and Christopher Jencks, "The Viability of the American College" in *The American College,* ed. R. Nevitt Sanford (New York: Wiley, 1962), p. 1953.

31. Cf. John D. Donovan, "The American Catholic Hierarchy: A Social Profile," *The American Catholic Sociological Review,* Vol. XIX (June 1958).

32. Hofstadter and Metzger, *op. cit.,* p. 352.

33. *Op. cit.,* pp. 204-205.

34. Hofstadter and Metzger, *op. cit.,* p. 352.

35. Talcott Parsons, *Structure and Process in Modern Societies* (Glencoe: The Free Press, 1960), pp. 307-308.

36. Cf. Congar, *op. cit.*

37. Some smaller Catholic colleges have lay presidents, but they are notable exceptions.

38. For a recent analysis of this problem, cf. Daniel Callahan, *The Mind of the Catholic Layman* (New York: Scribner, 1963).

CHAPTER 3

1. Representative studies include Logan Wilson, *The Academic Man;* W. L. Warner and James Abegglen, *Big Business Leaders in America* (New York: Harper, 1955); Mabel Newcomer, *The Big Business Executive: the Factors that Made Him, 1900-1950* (New York: Columbia University Press, 1955); Anne Roe, *The Making of a Scientist* (New York: Dodd, 1953).

2. There is no *a priori* basis for assuming that the religious and lay professors have such different social origins as to require separate analysis.

3. Lazarsfeld and Thielens, *op. cit.,* p. 438. It should be noted, however, that their sample included female as well as male professors from all types of colleges and universities.

4. This projection may understate the case because, unlike the layman, the clerical professor does not have to retire at sixty-five. On the contrary, the religious congregation must continue to support him and his "contributed services" constitute a sound financial reason for the college to use him in the classroom.

5. Faculty stability among the religious is a function of the limited range of assignments open to them within province boundaries. The stability

of the layman is variously related to personal considerations, to the high premium placed on institutional loyalty, and to some special restrictions on his market situation. The "Gentlemen's Agreement" among Jesuit colleges, for example, circumscribes their lay professors' market prospects by requiring that other Jesuit college administrators be advised in advance of any attempt to recruit lay members of their faculties.

6. Cf. Francis C. Madigan, "Role Satisfactions and Length of Life in a Closed Population," *American Journal of Sociology*, Vol. 67 (May 1962).

7. The data on the place of birth of grandparents describe only the *number* who were foreign-born or born in the United States.

8. Joseph H. Fichter, *Religion As an Occupation* (Notre Dame: University of Notre Dame Press, 1961), p. 66.

9. John W. Gustad, *The Career Decisions of College Teachers* (Atlanta: Southern Regional Education Board, 1960), p. 16; Ruth E. Eckert and John E. Stecklein, *Job Motivations and Satisfactions of College Teachers* (Washington: U.S. Dept. of Health, Education and Welfare, 1961), p. 11.

10. S. M. Lipset and R. Bendix, using data collected by Stouffer in his study of civil liberties, have calculated that non-manual occupations were held by only 30% of American Catholics who were foreign-born or the native-born sons of foreign-born fathers and by 38% of the native-born sons of native-born fathers. Cf. their *Social Mobility in Industrial Societies* (Berkeley: University of California Press, 1959), p. 50.

11. Lazarsfeld and Thielens, *op. cit.*, p. 6.

12. *Ibid.*, p. 7.

13. *Ibid.*

14. Cf. Fichter, *op. cit.*, pp. 35-36 for more detailed data concerning family size of seminarians.

15. *Ibid.*, p. 37. Fichter's seminarian sample was composed of only children or first-born in 33% of the cases.

16. Daniel R. Miller and Guy E. Swanson, *The Changing American Parent* (New York: Wiley, 1958); Gerhard Lenski, *The Religious Factor* (New York: Doubleday, 1961); Bernard C. Rosen, "The Achievement Syndrome: A Psychocultural Dimension of Social Stratification," *American Sociological Review*, Vol. 21 (1956); David C. McClelland, ed., *Studies in Motivation* (New York: Appleton-Century-Crofts, 1955).

17. *Ibid.*

18. Cf. William E. Henry, "The Business Executive: Dynamics of a Social Role," *The American Journal of Sociology*, Vol. 54 (January 1949).

19. Fichter, *op. cit.*, p. 22.

CHAPTER 4

1. Peter H. and Alice S. Rossi, "Some Effects of Parochial School Education in America," *Harvard Educational Review*, Vol. XXVII, No. 3 (Summer, 1957).
2. Fichter, *op. cit.;* Donovan, *op. cit.*
3. Rossi, *op. cit.*
4. Fichter reports that 80% of the seminarians had been altar boys. *Op. cit.*, p. 40.
5. *Ibid.*
6. Cf. Ruth E. Eckert and John E. Stecklein, *op. cit.*
7. *Ibid.*

CHAPTER 5

1. For a study descriptive of some of the processes at work in faculty mobility, cf. Caplow and McGee, *op. cit.*
2. At almost every college visited, AAUP Chapters were in the process of being established or revitalized.
3. The theme of "loyalty" has been a commonplace in the evaluation of the lay staff by religious administrators. Its quality as a virtue aside, the expectation of loyalty has conditioned some officials to perceive professional criticism as disloyal behavior.
4. The Lazarsfeld-Thielens index (*op. cit.*) was adapted for use here. Each professor was assigned a gross publishing index in the range of 0, 1, 2, 3, or 4 based upon the completion of a Ph.D. dissertation and the publication of books, monographs, and articles. Papers read at conventions were not included, as they were in the Lazarsfeld-Thielens study, in computing the publication indices of Catholic professors. It is unlikely that this difference seriously distorts the comparative picture.
5. Ellis, *op. cit.;* O'Dea, *op. cit.*
6. For an analysis of the strength of family ties among American Catholics as compared to Protestants and Jews, cf. Gerhard Lenski, *op. cit.*, pp. 192-233.

CHAPTER 6

1. These three measures were variously modeled after or adapted from the research instruments used by The National Opinion Research Center in its 1958 study of American graduate students directed by James Davis.
2. For a non-comparable description of the major satisfactions of a college teaching career among Minnesota faculty members, see Eckert and Stecklein, *op. cit.*, pp. 37-40.
3. Cf. McClelland's similar findings, *op. cit.*

CHAPTER 7

1. These "elite" professors were not part of the random sample. They are included only in the materials of this chapter for the reasons noted in the text.
2. *Op. cit.*
3. Ellis, *op. cit.*; O'Dea, *op. cit.*
4. The number of the professors who had a non-Catholic parent is, of course, so small that this relationship to publication performance is statistically insecure.
5. Lenski, *op. cit.*; Rosen, *op. cit.*; McClelland, *op. cit.*
6. O'Dea, *op. cit.*
7. Cf. Lenski, *op. cit.*; Miller and Swanson, *op. cit.*
8. *Ibid.*
9. *Op. cit.*

CHAPTER 8

1. Such graduate student help is available only in universities. In the competition for superior graduate students most Catholic universities are placed at a disadvantage by their lack of resources and less prestigious reputations.
2. For the major dissatisfactions of a college teaching career as reported by college faculty members in Minnesota, cf. Eckert and Stecklein, *op. cit.*, p. 43.
3. Less than 5% of the Minnesota sample indicated dissatisfaction with the absence of a policy-making role by the faculty. *Ibid.*

CHAPTER 9

1. The decisive difference between the extra-academic authority of political bodies and of religious superiors is the openness of the former to removal by democratic processes.
2. Cf. Callahan, *op. cit.*
3. Donovan, art. cit., "The American Catholic Hierarchy."
4. Most seminaries in the United States are separate institutions or have little intellectual contact with the other schools of the universities with which they are affiliated.

AAUP, 43, 94, 174, 226
Abegglen, James, 224
Academic careers, 88-97
  AAUP, 94
  career mobility of faculty, 88-97
  degree status, 90-94
  early paternalism, 96
  factors in initial appointments, 91-92
  institutional stability, 93-95
  market value, 95
  promotion policies, 96-97
  religious faculty, 88-89
  role of religious superiors, 88-89
Academic freedom, 181-182
  faculty satisfaction, 181
  Index of Forbidden Books, 29
  perceived by faculty, 182
  perceived by non-Catholics, 182
  status of, 182
Academic rank, distribution in sample, 12
  promotion policies, 96-97

Academic rank (*Continued*)
  relationship to publication, 138-140
  relationship to value orientations, 138-140
Administration of Catholic colleges, 30-32, 42-43, 121, 170-175
  Church law, 30-33
  dean, 43, 173
  departmental chairman, 173
  lay participation, 173-175
  president, 28, 31, 42
  religious structure and policies, 170-175
  religious superior, 30-32
  role preference of faculty for, 121
  trustees, 43
  vice-president, 43
Affective ties of professor to parents, 62-63
  relationship to publication, 159-160
Age of faculty, 48-50
  age composition of sample, 48

Age of faculty (*Continued*)
    implications of age composition, 49-50
Altar boys, 71
    academic man as, 71
    priestly vocation from, 71
American Catholic Historical Society, 102
American higher education, 36-44
    See also Catholic higher education
    dynamics of, 36-44
    early religious structure of, 38, 40
    evolution of university in, 37-40
Associations, professional, 102-103
    Catholic, 102
    faculty participation in, 103
    national, 102
Attwater, Donald, 223
Authoritarian family structure, 60-62, 158-160
    relationship to publication, 158-160
    relationship to value orientation, 145
Authority-figure in families, 61-63
    relationship to professional values, 145
    relationship to publication, 223

Bendix, R., 225
Benedictines, 33, 34, 36
Bishops, jurisdiction *re* Catholic colleges, 29-30, 173
    intellectual orientation of, 29-**30**

Bowler, Sr. Mary M., 222, 223
Bradburn, Norman, 221
Brim, Orville G., 221
Brown-Pembroke, 28

Callahan, Daniel, 224, 227
Canon law, 29
Caplow, Theodore, 5, 221, 226
Career satisfactions, 117-120
    perceived by lay professors, 118-119
    perceived by religious professors, 118-119
    rank ordering of, 117-118
Cassidy, Francis P., 222
Catholic Comission on Intellectual and Cultural Affairs, The, viii, 222
Catholic higher education, 16-44, 178-180, 189-205
    See also American higher education, Administration, Bishops, Canon law, Religious superiors
    AAUP in, 43
    Catholic university development, 38-39
    changing religious and lay roles in, 197-201
    faculty evolution of, 22-25
    financial problems of, 178-180
    history of, 16-25
    intellectual goals of nineteenth century, 18
    recruitment problems, 202
    relationship of Church traditions, 26-29

Catholic higher education (*Cont.*)
relative to dynamics of American education, 36-44
religious structure of, 25-44, 190-191
resistance to secularization in, 40-44
"rule" and "spirit" of congregation, 33-34, 35
"spirit" of congregation and lay professors, 34
status of lay professors, 203-204
sub-culture of American Catholicism, 34-36
summary facts, 189-193
summary problems, 193-201
summary projections, 201-205
women's colleges, 21-22
Catholic intellectual, 6-10
research definition of, 7-9
Christ, Frank L., 222
College education of professors, 75-80
evaluation of education, 79
factors in choice of college, 78-79
relationship to publication, 164-168
relationship to value orientation, 146-148
seminary education, 76-78
type of college, 78-79
Columbia University, 37
Columbia-Barnard, 28
Congar, Yves M.J., 223-224
Congregation for the Propagation of the Faith, 223
Conventions, attendance, 103

Davis, James A., 221, 226
Doctoral degree, relationship to publication, 166-167
Dominicans, 33, 34
Donovan, John D., 224, 227

Ecclesiastical legislation, relationship to Catholic higher education, 29-33
Eckert, Ruth, 54, 82, 225, 226, 227
Ecological origins of the faculty, 50-51
degree of regional stability, 50
urban concentration, 50-51
Educational values of parents, 64-65
relationship to faculty publication, 160
types of values, 64-65
Elementary school education of professor, 68-73
academic achievements, 70
faculty evaluations, 72-73
relationship to publication, 162-164
relationship to value orientations, 146-148
type of school, 68-71
Ellis, John T., 6, 8, 155, 221, 226, 227
Erbacher, Sebastian A., 222, 223
Extra-curricular duties of academic man, 99-101
by religious or lay status, 99-101

Extra-curricular duties of academic man (*Continued*)
  time expended per week, 99-101
  types of activities, 100-101

Facilities and services for professors, institutional, 177-180
  clerical assistance, 180
  laboratories, 177-178
  libraries, 177-178
  offices, 178-179
Family backgrounds of the faculty, 51-58
  Irish family system, 52
  nationality, 52
  parental education, 53-54
  parental income, 57
  parental origins, 51-53
  parental religion, 54-55
  paternal occupation, 55-57
  relationship to publication, 154-160
  relationship to value orientations, 140-145
  social class, 57
  social mobility, 56-57
  socio-economic status, 55-58
  style of family, 59-60
Family of lay professors, 109-111
  age at marriage, 109
  degree status at marriage, 109
  number of children, 109
  relationship to profession, 109-110
  wife's education, 109
Fichter, Joseph H., 54, 59, 65, 74, 225, 226

Georgetown University, 19
G.I. Bill, significance of, 193
  for Catholic colleges, 193
  for faculty growth, 92-93
Goldsen, Rose, 221
Goodrich, H.B., 221
Graduate school education of professors, 80-84
  clerical attendance, 80
  degree attainment, 81-83
  evaluation of graduate program by degree levels, 83-84
  interrupted study, 84
  factors in choice, 80-81
  professionalization of Catholic faculty, 82-83
  relationship to publication, 165-168
  relationship to value orientations, 146-148
Greenbaum, J.J., 154, 221
Gross, Neal, 221
Gustad, John W., 54, 82, 225

Harvard University, 37, 41
Harvard-Radcliffe, 28
Henry, William E., 159, 225
High school education of professor, 73-75
  aspiration to priesthood, 73-74
  relationship of size of school, 74
  relationship to publication, 162-164
  relationship to value orientations, 146-148
  type of school, 73
Hofstadter, Richard, 21, 223, 224

Humanities, professors of, 12, 138-139, 152-153
  number in sample, 12
  publication indices, 152-153
  value orientations, 138-139

Index of Forbidden Books, 29, 224
Instructors, number in sample, 11-12
  publications indices, 104, 151-168
  value orientations, 115-149
Irish influence, 191-192

Jencks, Christopher, 31, 224
Jesuits, 33, 34, 36, 77, 84, 201, 225
Jewish families, 61-62
Jews, 40

Knapp, R.H., 154, 221

Large colleges, 139, 153-154, 222
  definition, 222
  faculty composition, 153
  number in sample, 153
  relationship to publication, 153-154
  relationship to value orientation, 139
Lawler, Justus, 7, 221
Lay professors, administrative opportunities, 42-43
  historical evolution of, 23-24
  number in sample, 12
  professionalization of education, 171-175

Lay professors (*Continued*)
  professional satisfactions of, 183-184
  professional status of, 90-91
  prototype of laity in Church, 27-28
  relationship to religious professors, 183
  role preferences of, 122
  secondary vocations, 92
  teaching satisfactions of, 118-119
  value-conflict decisions of, 131-133
Lazarsfeld, Paul, 48, 58, 104, 105, 221, 224, 225, 226
Lenski, Gerhard, 61, 62, 110, 157, 158, 225, 226, 227
Lipset, S.M., 225
Lutherans, 40

McClelland, David, 157, 158, 225, 226, 227
McGee, Reece J., 5, 221, 226
Madigan, Francis C., 225
Medium-sized colleges, definition, 222
  faculty composition, 153
  number in sample, 153
  relationship to publication, 153-154
  relationship to value orientation, 139
Merton, Robert K., 221
Metzger, Walter P., 37, 223, 224
Miller, Daniel, 61, 110, 225, 227

National Opinion Research Center, 226
Natural Science, professors of, number in sample, 12
  publication indices, 152-153
  value orientations, 138-139
Newcomer, Mabel, 224
Non-Catholic academicians, 88-94
  images of Catholic colleges, 94
  recruitment of, 88-89
  silence of comparable data, 93
Non-Catholic family backgrounds, 61-62
  conversions, 55
  number in sample, 55
  relationship to publication, 156-157
  relationship to value orientations, 143-144

O'Dea, Thomas F., 78, 155, 157, 221, 222, 226, 227
Official Directory of Catholic Colleges and Universities, The, 222, 223
Ong, Walter, 25, 191

Parental education, 53-54
  levels of attainment, 53-54
  relationship to publication, 155
  relationship to faculty value orientations, 141-142
Parental religion, 54-55, 63
  degree of intensity, 63
  relationship to publication, 156-157
  relationship to value orientation, 143-145

Parental values and influences, 58-65
  affective ties, 62-63
  authoritarian family structure, 60-62
  authority-figure, 61-63
  educational values, 64-65
  family atmosphere, 60
  family size, 59-60
  maternal role, 62-63
  relationship to publication, 154-160
  relationship to value orientation, 140-145
  religious tone, 63
Parochial school education, 68-73
  evaluation by professors, 72-73
  proportion attending, 162
  relationship to publication, 162-164
  relationship to value orientations, 146-148
Parsons, Talcott, 40, 43, 224
Paternal occupation, 55-57
  relationship to publication, 155-156
  relationship to value orientations, 142
  type of occupation, 56
Power, Edward, 18, 19, 38, 222, 223
Princeton University, 37
Professionalization of Catholic faculty, 82-83
Professional role
  See Role, professional
  See also Value orientations

Professors, 12, 138-139
  number in sample, 12
  value orientations of, 138-139
Professors, assistant, 12, 138-139
  number in sample, 12
  value orientations of, 138-139
Professors, associate, 12, 138-139
  number in sample, 12
  value orientations of, 138-139
Publication, 103-105, 151-168
  affective ties and, 159-160
  authoritarian family structure, 158-160
  authority-figure of family, 159-160
  basis of publication index, 104-105, 151
  compared with Lazarsfeld-Thielens sample, 104-105
  composition of publishing and non-publishing sub-groups, 151-168
  family structure and, 157-160
  region of college and, 153-154
  relationship of higher education, 164-168
  relationship to Catholic or non-Catholic college and university education, 164-166
  relationship to degree status, 164-166
  relationship to elementary school background, 162-164
  relationship to family socialization, 154-160
  relationship to high school educational background, 162-164

Publication (*Continued*)
  relationship to parental education, 155
  relationship to parental religion, 156-157
  relationship to paternal occupation, 155-156
  relationship to work load, 176
  religious-lay differential, 103-105, 152-154
  religious professors, 108
  school socialization, 160-168
  size of college, 153-154
  statistical record of, 104
  subject area, 152-154
Publication index, 104-105, 151
  compared, 104-105
  limitations, 151

Religious superiors, 30-32
  dual role of religious faculty, 31-32
  effect on career appointment and mobility, 88-89
  lay faculty, 32, 197-199
  tenure of office, 31
Research design, 11, 12, 13
Research-oriented professor, 120-124, 132-135, 136-138, 140-148, 176-177
Research, preference for, 120-124, 132-135, 136-138, 140-148
Research-publication orientation, Catholic universities, 39
Research universe, 8, 9, 10
Riesman, David, 27, 31, 224
Roe, Anne, 224

Role-conflict, priest-professor, 106, 107

Role preferences, 120-124
  See also Value orientations

Role, professional, 105-108
  family compared to non-Catholic professor, 110
  family responsibilities and, 106, 109-110
  family situation and, 109-110
  lay professor, 106, 109-110
  priest and publication, 108
  priest-professor, 104-106, 107-108
  role conflict, 106, 107

Rooney, William J., ix

Rosen, Bernard, 61, 157, 225, 227

Rossi, Alice, 69, 70, 226

Rossi, Peter, 69, 70, 226

St. Mary's College (Baltimore), 19

Sample, 8-13
  components of, 11-12
  data collection, 12
  limitations of, 8-10, 12-13
  random selection procedure, 12
  refusals, 12
  representativeness, 8-9, 12
  size of, 11-12
  substitution procedure, 11-12
  universe used, 8-10

Secularization of American higher education, 40-44, 192
  resistance of Catholic leaders, 42, 192
  theology and philosophy, 41-42, 194-195

Seminary education of religious professor, 75-80

Sherry, Gerard E., 222

Small colleges, 139, 153-154, 222
  definition, 222
  faculty composition, 153
  relationship to publication, 153-154
  relationship to value orientation, 139

Socialization of the faculty, 47-65
  See Family, Elementary school, High school, College

Social origins of the faculty
  See Family backgrounds, parental, paternal

Social science, professors of, 12, 138-139, 152-153
  number in sample, 12
  publication indices, 152-153
  value orientations, 138-139

"Spirit" of religious congregations, 33-34, 35
  implication for lay professors, 34

Stecklein, John E., 54, 82, 225, 226, 227

Stouffer, Samuel, 56

Swanson, Guy E., 61, 110, 225, 227

Teaching loads, 98-99

Teaching oriented professors, 121, 122-124, 132-135, 136-138, 140-148, 176-177

Teaching role, preference for, 121, 122-124, 132-135, 136-138, 140-148

Teaching satisfactions, 117-120
Tewksbury, Donald George, 21
Theology and philosophy, 40-42,
171-172, 194-195, 202-203
effect on work situation, 171-
172
problem of, 194-195
secularization and, 40-42, 202-
203
Thielens, Wagner, 48, 58, 104,
105, 221, 224, 225, 226
Tradition, effect on Catholic
higher education, 26-29

University of Chicago, 37, 41
University of California, 37, 41

Value-conflict situations, 119,
124-135
Value orientations, 115-149, 176-
177
administration, preference for,
122
authority-figure in family, 145
individual, 136-138
intellectual over moral, 117-119
moral obligations, 131
moral orientation, 119
parental education, 141-142
parental religion, 143-145
paternal occupation, 142
relationship to family socialization, 140-145
relationship to school socialization, 146-148
research preference, 121-124,
132-135, 136-138, 140-148
role preferences, 120-124

Value orientations (*Continued*)
teaching preference, 121, 122-
124, 132-135, 136-138, 140-
148
teaching satisfactions, 117-120
value conflict, 119, 124-135
value-orientation profile, 123-
124
work load, 176-177
Van Tassel, John, x
Veblen, Thorstein, 5, 221
Vocations, 71, 92
altar boy factor, 71
secondary vocation for some lay
professors, 92

Warner, W. L., 224
Wilson, Logan, 5, 221, 224
Women's colleges, Catholic, 21-
22, 201
Work load of the faculty, 97-101,
175-177
effect on work situation, 175-
177
effect on publication, 176
non-class loads, 99-101
class loads, 98-99
Work situation, 169-185
AAUP, 174
administration policies and
practices, 170-175
authority-figure, 173
criticism of religiously-oriented
policies, 172
ecclesiastical rule, 172-173
evaluation, 180-185
facilities, 177-180

Work situation (*Continued*)
   financial problem, 178-180
   frustrations, 183-184
   layman and administration, 173-175
   publication, 176
   relationship to theology and philosophy, 171-172

Work situation (*Continued*)
   religious character of administrative policies, 170-175
   research, 176-177
   satisfactions, 181-183
   work loads, 175-177

Yale University, 37